PUSHING WATER UPHILL
With A Rake

Memoirs of a Successful Failure

By

STEVE BAKER

For information about purchasing books
in quantities for organizations or sales
promotions, please contacting publisher at
MerricPublishing@earthlink.net.

Published in the United States of America by Merric
Publishing

Email Steve Baker at PushingWaterUphill@earthlink.net

ISBN: 0-9761695-0-9
Category: 1. Business   2. Self Help

*"Not only a riveting roller coaster ride
of a story; Steve has written a how-to book
for business and life."*
— Steve Bathgate, President/CEO, Bathgate Capital Partners

*"Full of great ideas.
You'll want to read it again with a highlighter."*
— Robert M. Martinez, President/CEO, MKTG Corporate Partners

*"A powerful real-life story that puts a
human face on success and failure in the
competitive world of business.*
— Robert J. Amedeo, Chief Operating Officer, Altegris Investments

*"In the aftermath of current business
scandals, this is a very timely, topical,
and interesting book."*
— Dale Rasmussen, CEO
Quantum Fuel Systems Technologies Worldwide

*"Thank you for writing this book. Our family
business is going into financial ruin and all
communication had shut down between us.
Your book opened a much needed conversation
that will help us get through the
toughest time in our lives.*
— Name withheld by request

Acknowledgments

If it takes two accounting firms to add up all of your assets, but you can count your friends on one hand...well, you do the math.

While I was writing this book, I was surrounded by encouraging family members and many friends who pushed, prodded, cajoled, criticized, and, above all, supported me. My thanks go to the following:

Profound thanks to my wife Marcia, son Eric, daughter Merridy and son-in-law Michael. Thank you for your love and faith in me, I am blessed to have you as my family.

Rob Johnson of Wilson/Johnson Creative, who used his skills, talent and, as always, his patience with me while designing the book's layout, design, and cover.

Ed Larkin and Dave Drennen, best friends and rotten golf partners. (O.K., great golf partners who play as poorly as I do.) Your belief in me and your support made the difference.

Bill and Teri Padget, partners, friends, and fellow survivors.

Ruth Ann Bearden, my editor, who helped put my words in order.

All of the incredible employees of WorldGroup who inspired this book. I smile every time I think of each of you. You were the very best.

In loving memory of
Mae Baker,
Mom and Grandma
Extraordinaire

1

A Shaky Start

A h, Ixtapa, Mexico! It took us twelve hours, but we had finally arrived. As my partner Ben and I stood in line to check into the gorgeous new Westin resort, we felt the warm pacific breeze flow through the open air lobby. We breathed in the moist aroma of the thick flora surrounding us and plotted which tequila drinks we would attack first. It was a beautiful Mexican evening in September, 1985.

Our conversation was abruptly interrupted by a sound that didn't quite mesh with the environment. At first, I thought it was faint thunder coming from the ocean, but the early evening was clear and bright. Before I could say a word, a low, deep growling, grinding rumble began and I knew this wasn't thunder. In a matter of seconds, the ground started shaking and the screaming began. As we stood frozen in fear, the shaking intensified and in a few more brief seconds, it had grown so strong that both people and objects started falling around us.

The Mexican employees screamed, "Terremoto, Terremoto!." Then, with a shaking arm, the hotel manager pointed everyone toward a hallway, while shouting, "Temblor de tierra de gran intensidad! Salga ahora! SALGA

AHORA!" The result of this proclamation was like a gun shot in the middle of a cattle herd, and the stampede began. People were screaming, pushing and jostling each other in confused chaos toward the exits – wherever the hell the exits were. The hallway that we had all chosen for our escape route was about fifteen feet wide and immediately became jammed with people frantic to escape. Ben and I tried to keep by the wall, but in a single instant, the inertia of so many bodies trying to reach safety created a rushing human wave of terror. We were sucked into the wave, and were being swept away with the hysterical horde.

It was around 7:00 p.m. Many women were dressed for dinner, and high heels did not make good running shoes. Men and women alike were falling down and getting trampled by this stampeding herd of so-called humanity. I caught sight of a lady in a bright pink dress about twenty feet in front of us and, in an instant, she disappeared. I shouted to Ben, and a few seconds later, Ben and I were over her. She had been knocked down and was being run over. We attempted to stop to help her up, but were both hit from behind and pushed forward. We grabbed her by her arms and dragged her along with us for nearly twenty feet until we could pull her to her feet. We wrapped her arms around our necks and continued trying to run with the wave. If we had tried to slow down or stop, the three of us would have been slammed to the ground.

People were collapsing from the combination of the stampede and the violent shaking of the floor. Then, to make matters worse, chunks of walls and ceiling started falling from above, increasing the number of injured people in the path of panic.

Finally, after what seemed an eternity, we made it outside. Once outside, the masses scattered in all directions in a desperate attempt to escape injury. In the dimming light of dusk, Ben and I continued running away from the hotel, carrying our new friend along with us. As we ran, I kept looking back — and up — trying to gauge how far away safety would be if the whole building started to come down onto our path of escape. At the same time, we had to watch where we were going because the parking area that we were running across was made of softball sized river stones, and as if that didn't make the footing bad enough, the surface was cracking and small fissures were opening around us.

People were running in all directions, still screaming from pain or fear, and calling out for missing friends. We heard someone scream, "Oh my God, it's Julie!" Our lady in pink was spotted by the friends who had left her behind in their own run for survival. For the first time, we knew who we had saved. Julie had a badly twisted ankle, a three inch cut on her forehead and blood dripping from the edge of her swollen lip. She would also have bruises all over her body tomorrow, courtesy of people's feet. Julie's dress was torn from her right shoulder down to her waist, and she had lost her shoes, but she sure looked great to her friends. We got quick introductions, hugs and sobbing thank yous. They had other friends to find and seconds later we separated, never to see each other again.

Ben and I continued running in our search of a safe haven. About two hundred yards from the hotel, we found a stand of small trees on a hill that appeared to be our refuge. We finally stopped for the first time to catch our breath. We stood there in momentary solitude, breathing deeply, not saying a word. In our silence, we could hear the continuing cries of desperate human distress along with the sounds of walls and other objects breaking and crashing to the ground.

I took a few more deep breaths then asked, "So Ben, how's your Spanish?"

"Not good, why?"

"I was wondering what that hotel guy was screaming back there, something like, "Temblor de tierra de gran intensidad?"

We looked at each other and instantly broke out laughing with the answer – "One big flipping earthquake!"

This couldn't be a major earthquake – not again. The earthquake hit just thirty six hours before and wiped out parts of Mexico City. And that was Mexico City, and we were here in Ixtapa, far southwest on the Pacific coast. When the Mexico City earthquake hit, we had watched the news and called the airline, which informed us that our flight was still on. If the first earthquake had not been over, we wouldn't have left Denver over twelve hours ago. We quickly realized that it wasn't over, good old Mother Nature was just beginning round two, and evidently she had just been waiting for us to arrive.

I looked at Ben, and joked, halfheartedly, "Well, partner, this is one hell of a way to start the most important business conference of our lives."

Ben shook his head in nervous amusement and replied, "Well, you said that you were going to give them a presentation that would knock 'em over. What do you have for an encore?" We laughed, took more deep breaths, and then once again stood in silence, surveying the scene before us.

With all of the distractions unfolding around us, I had almost forgotten why we were here in beautiful Ixtapa, Mexico. Ben and I were here to solidify a big business contract with a major company, and this convention at this stunning resort was going to be the kick off.

Back in the fall of 1984, my partner Ben and I decided to embark upon a new adventure. We had previously started a successful financial management software company which was sold to a major airline. After two years in a large corporate airline bureaucracy, we decided to begin anew. We knew the travel industry and we knew software and this would be the foundation of our new company, Global Group. (Sure, we had lofty ideas.)

Two guys in our thirties, Ben and I worked well together. Ben was trained as a CPA and had a great business vision and financial sense. He knew numbers inside and out and knew how to work them. Coming from a military family, he was also well disciplined to get plans implemented and completed. But he was also a contradiction of terms. At six feet and 190 pounds, he was still the good athlete who had gone to college on a baseball scholarship. Ben knew business, but he also knew how to have a great time in life. Growing up a Navy brat, he had a passion for sailing and loved a good drink. He was a CPA with a "work hard – play hard" view on life.

I was the creative right-brainer that had the absolute passion and skills to build any marketing and sales program. I also had strong people skills and an intuitive knack for finding the finest employees to help a company grow. With me, it was "what you see is what you get." I was quite simply a marketing guy that loved life and the people in it. I enjoyed life and living it to the max.

We had moved to Evergreen, Colorado from the Midwest to start our previous company, and lived together for six months before we could move our families out. We knew each other's strengths and weaknesses in business and life, and had become best friends.

Ben would be President/ CEO and I would be Executive Vice President. Some thought of us as two cocky young guys, but we saw ourselves as merely having supreme confidence. We knew we weren't the two smartest guys on the planet, but we also knew we had the work ethic, positive attitude, brass onions, and pit bull persistence to accomplish anything. We sincerely knew who we were and where we were headed.

In his book *Management*, Peter Drucker stated it plainly,

"There is only one valid definition of business: to create a customer...and the business enterprise has only two basic functions: Marketing and Innovation."

With that in mind, we took a very serious "Think – Plan – Do" approach to our business plan and developed four goals:

<u>First</u>, create a product that was uniquely beneficial to the travel industry.

<u>Second</u>, create the strongest and most efficient means of sales and distribution.

<u>Third</u>, take the company public as soon as possible to raise the capital necessary to build a strong profitable business that future competitors couldn't touch.

<u>Fourth</u>, sell the company in three years for a boatload of cash. This would benefit not only Ben and me, but all of our future employees and investors. It would also allow Ben to sail around the world while I would go play golf.

We had the right plan and our investment capital from selling our previous company, so we rolled up our sleeves, got out our check books and in January 1985 we started Global

Group, Inc.

In the 80's there was no readily available source of information about hotels and resorts to help travel agencies book leisure travel. There were mainly books and catalogs which were incomplete and out of date. Travel agents actually had to get on the phone to book a property for their customers. The major airlines had automated reservation systems to book airline travel but were just beginning to add large corporate hotels to their data bases. These were pre-internet days, so there were no such resources as "www.bookatrip.coms." Our research showed that the industry was ready and eager for a reliable source of information that they could access via a computer, and they were willing to pay for good information.

After exhaustive market research, we decided to build the first automated information and reservation system for leisure travel. It would be an interactive data base of information about hotels and resorts around the world and we would offer it to the 27,000 travel agencies in the United States on a subscription basis. Once we got going, the properties would also pay us listing fees and commissions for bookings.

On the entrepreneur "Risk/Return Ratio" our conservative projections showed a positive cash flow in two years, and was well deserving of our time and capital investments. So we started hiring the programming staff to begin building the foundation for LeisureLink, the Leisure Travel System.

While Ben stayed on top of the project of writing the programs to make the thing work, I got on the road to build the data base of information about the properties. Since Global Group was based in Evergreen, Colorado, we decided that our first target market would be all of the ski resorts, Bed & Breakfasts, dude ranches and hotels throughout the Rocky Mountain area. I packed up my car and took off throughout every corner of Colorado and Utah. I did one-on-one pitches, and larger presentations to hotel associations, tourist boards, and anyone else that would listen to our story and sign up for LeisureLink. In two months we had a very complete data base of information about resort properties in Colorado and Utah.

LeisureLink was designed to provide complete and detailed information that would enable travel agencies to make vacation bookings. Each property listing contained seventy fields of information. When I returned, we started the task of manually loading each property into the computers and then came the long but necessary testing of the system. By late summer, after some major and minor tweaking, LeisureLink actually worked!

Our next resort target was the Caribbean. I know what you're thinking, that it was tough duty, but someone had to do it. I had worked with the Caribbean Hotel Association in the past and had established a solid business network. From Nassau, south to Barbados, I traveled throughout the Caribbean islands presenting our program and signing up resorts and properties. We had the majority of the Caribbean properties signed on, and by August we were loading all of the new data into LeisureLink, continually testing along the way.

We were now ready to move to the next part of the equation: distribution and sales. It was time to demonstrate LeisureLink to the travel industry and start signing up subscribers.

There are warehouses and junkyards full of great products that never got to market. Whether the product is a car, a computer, or this book that you're reading, success comes down to this: without a strong distribution and sales network, even a great product is heading for a landfill. For many products and services, the fastest way to build strong distribution and sales is to become a "preferred supplier" with companies that already have a customer base.

We went after a preferred supplier target to help us get big, fast. We approached one of the oldest and largest travel agency franchisors in the country. International Travel Partners (ITP) had 230 locations and did $300 million in annual revenues. Franchisors make their money not only by selling franchise licenses, but also by providing products and services to their franchisees. They search out vendors and then they make a piece of whatever their franchisees buy from these vendors. We offered LeisureLink to ITP.

The program would work like this: ITP would

promote us to their franchisees as a trusted preferred supplier, and we would offer LeisureLink to the franchisees at a discount. We would then pay a commission back to ITP headquarters for every agency that signed up. We put together a comprehensive plan to promote LeisureLink to the agencies in regional meetings, and were invited to do a major presentation at their annual convention in Ixtapa, Mexico.

☆☆☆☆☆☆☆☆☆☆

The earth shook me back to reality…Ixtapa, Mexico, in the middle of an earthquake! Ben and I had worked too hard and spent too much money to get this far and be denied our opportunity for incredible success. We would make it through this.

It had been about an hour since we started our ordeal and it was past dusk. With all electricity was gone, our only source of light was the moon, which luckily was almost full. People began to meander back toward the hotel looking for friends and seeking answers. We thought that this was not a good idea if aftershocks should start, so we stayed where we were for awhile. We sat and watched dazed people walking around aimlessly, with no place to go. The place looked like a mini war zone, with chunks of concrete, strange smells, walking wounded, confusion and despair. After awhile, Ben and I decided to carefully head back toward the hotel to see if we could locate some of the group of travel agency people that we were there to meet.

Maneuvering our way through the debris, we made it near the front of the hotel and saw some people that we knew. We yelled and got their attention, and started heading towards them. However, before we could reach them, the first major aftershock started and triggered the whole panic scene again. People once again screamed and scattered for safety. It would take another hour before we started to regroup.

It was now pushing 9:00 p.m. and we finally got together with the others and started exchanging our stories. Fortunately, we found out that no one in the resort was critically injured. We decided that if another aftershock hit that we would all head for our grove of trees which I aptly named "Steve's Sanctuary."

We began to relax a bit and were enjoying our conversation with the group of ITP travel agency owners until, like clockwork, another even stronger shock hit around 10:00 p.m. We all ran to my sanctuary and conversation was once again traded for concern and anxiety. Okay, adventure is one thing, but this was already getting old. How long was Mother Earth going to toy with us?

As our environment once again calmed down, we began to think about declaring victory. It was almost 11:30 p.m. and nothing new had happened. The resort managers began to call out for everyone to approach the front of the hotel. The crowds carefully stepped closer, always ready to turn and run in an instant. The manager announced that they had done a building inspection and that the structure was deemed unsafe to reenter. That didn't really break our hearts, because Ben and I had never checked in, so our bags were still at the bag stand. That was the good news, the bad news was that the bag stand was buried in debris.The manager went on to explain that, barring another aftershock, the employees would bring out tables and then bring food and drink from the kitchen and bar. He pleaded for everyone to please be patient and we would all be served at a safe distance from the building as soon as possible. Ben and I watched in anger and disgust as people started to complain about their personal pains and discomfort, the lack of electricity or phones, and how they didn't come all this way "to be treated like this," and on and on, ad nausea. Here was this friendly staff that had their own families to worry about, and yet they were here earning a living by taking care of this ungrateful bunch of assholes.

Ben and I got a dozen of our new found friends and went to the manager with our offer to help his overburdened and stressed out staff. We got busy with them for the next hour, running in and out of the hotel with tables, and all the food and drink we could carry. We brought out everything from caviar and Champagne to white bread and peanut butter. The staff also ran in and out with blankets and pillows to comfort the guests. When everything was set up, it looked like a four star refugee camp.

12:30 a.m. found the area quiet, except for the sound of the tourists devouring everything and clamoring for more. It was as if the earthquake was giving us a dinner break, because shortly after 1:00 a.m. the aftershocks started again and continued throughout the night like clockwork. The only safe place to lie down was on the river stone parking area, so needless to say no one got much sleep. Ben and I just wandered around talking with people, while waiting for the next aftershock. At 4:30 a.m. a shock came but it wasn't from the ground.

Four Jeeps full of armed men roared up the drive to the resort and screeched to a halt in the parking lot in the middle of all of us. Looking ominous in dark pants and t-shirts and carrying rifles, they jumped from the vehicles and spread out in front of us. Ben leaned over to me and whispered, "Oh, this is just flipping great, we survive an earthquake just to be robbed and shot by banditos."

Enjoying his authority, the leader of the group strutted back and forth and began shouting orders to us. Yeah, like we understood Spanish. We stood there and replied, "Huh?" This new event was adding insult to injury and was too much to bear. Many of the tourists began to cry, while others began to throw their wallets and purses down at the feet of the armed men. A few minutes later, the hotel manager came forward with his bull horn to announce that these men were actually a local militia group that had been called out to check on us and assure our security. He also informed us that more militia would be dispatched sometime the next day to evacuate us to Acapulco. As the tourists sighed in relief and began to retrieve their belongings, Ben and I headed for the liquor table and a found a large soothing bottle of tequila.

The next afternoon, more militia began pulling in to begin the evacuation. They were driving anything that they could find. There were a few nice buses, but mostly it was old pickup trucks, and even older school buses. Group after group loaded up and headed for the trip south to Acapulco. Ben and I had to locate our buried luggage, so we were among the final few groups to evacuate, and at 1:00 p.m. we boarded an old school bus with no windows or front door. But that didn't matter as long as it ran and could make the one hundred thirty mile trip to safety. We tied luggage to the top, and loaded as many people as possible inside. In what resembled a scene from *Gandhi*, we were crammed three to four people in a seat that would normally seat two kids, while the aisle bulged with people standing.

As our mobile can of sardines began our exodus, we were grateful that there were no windows. Sardines probably smelled better than the people on our bus. There had been no showers for two days and the sweat was pouring down our bodies. But, what the heck, we could tolerate this for a few hours, because we'd be standing under a cool shower by 4:00 p.m. Yeah, right.

The one and only road connecting us to Acapulco had severe damage and we constantly had to get off the bus and push it through areas where the road had collapsed, and our old bus overheated five times. Finally at 3:00 a.m., a mere fourteen hours later, we pulled into the grand old Acapulco Princess Resort. We got our rooms and long showers, and in total fatigue and relief, slept until noon.

After my "nap" and another long shower, I headed to the lobby where I bought a newspaper. For the first time I understood what we had been through. We had indeed been part of the same band of earthquakes that hit Mexico City. The epicenter had been about 30 miles off the Mexican coast in the Pacific Ocean. It moved in a straight line to Mexico City, and in its path, was Ixtapa. This had been one of the strongest earthquakes throughout history. With an impact of 8.1 on the Richter Scale, the force was so strong that it had shaken buildings in Houston, Texas. The major devastation occurred in Mexico City, where over 20,000 people were killed and 100,000 more were left homeless. In comparison, we had been merely inconvenienced.

Miraculously, the next morning, International Travel Partners actually got their meeting started, and we did our presentation of LeisureLink. The bonding that had been created over the last forty eight hours was actually a gift, and 100% of the travel agency owners signed up for our service. No one looked upon us as vendors; we were now like a part of the ITP family, which would prove extremely valuable in the future.

The rest of the week was spent in celebration of life, and we enjoyed the best that Acapulco had to offer. By day we lounged by the pool and the beach and went snorkeling and boating. By night we feasted on exotic Mexican dishes that stunned and delighted our taste buds. We partied the nights away and attempted, but failed to drink Mexico out of tequila.

While Ben and I were flying home to our families, we toasted our adventure. "Well, partner", said Ben, "Our little company just survived trial by earthquake. If God decided not to stop us, nothing else will. Here's to our future, there's no stopping us now!"

Unfortunately, while we had been celebrating, our families back in Colorado had no idea if we were dead or alive because all phone lines were down. It wasn't until five days after the quake that we could get a flight to Houston and to a telephone where we could finally call home. When my wife answered and I said hello, she and the kids started screaming with joy and crying from relief, knowing for the first time that I was alive. I felt rather guilty about the fun that we had in Acapulco while they went through their own hell waiting for word of my existence. When I got home that night, there was a big "Welcome Home" banner hanging outside, and hugs, tears, and family love waiting inside.

☆☆☆☆☆☆☆☆☆☆

Once back to the office, we enjoyed local and regional celebrity status with newspaper and television interviews. Our "ordeal" gave us the added exposure that we needed in a public relations campaign to continue building new preferred supplier relationships to further our rapid growth.

The competition between the airlines owned reservation systems was fierce and they were each looking for an edge. Taking advantage of these conditions, we approached them with an offer to provide LeisureLink through their automated reservation systems as an exclusive value added service to their travel agency customers.

We flew around the country, meeting with major airlines, getting polite smiles and nods. All of the airlines looked at what we were doing, but we knew that many of them thought they would just knock us off.

We met with TWA who owned the PARS reservation information system. Our initial meeting was held in their offices in New York and was positive and productive. It was our strategy to have the second meeting in our small office in Evergreen, Colorado. Two weeks later TWA sent their reservation center managers and the vice president of marketing out to see our program first hand.

There was an advantage to having our company located in Evergreen, a beautiful little mountain town close to Denver. We could pick up the "big city folks" at the airport and in one hour be sitting in an area surrounded by mountains. Our picturesque setting became a great marketing tool that helped us get agreements signed. In our previous company, we closed many deals with major national and international airlines and travel companies with the help of Colorado. We planned to do the same thing with TWA.

Here's how it worked. The first day was spent in nonstop meetings and discussions, working straight through lunch. We then broke early in the afternoon and took our guests to an early dinner at our favorite restaurant. This historical old octagonal log structure was once a stagecoach station and now sat by the lake on Evergreen Golf Course. We lounged outside on the patio which was ten feet from the first tee box, a short par three that hit across rushing Bear Creek.

As we relaxed under the Colorado blue sky and warm sunshine, surrounded by mountains and sipping Coors beer, hard negotiations become softer. We talked business, interspersed with conversations of golf and Colorado skiing. The next morning, after intense and very convincing business discussions on our part, TWA's representatives were in agreement that we should be working together for sound business reasons. We took another early break and loaded everyone into a Suburban and drove them to the top of the world. Only an hour's drive from our office was Mt. Evans, an awesome mountain peak and home to the highest paved road in all of North America. This is a spectacular drive of switchback curves with 500 foot drop-offs and no guardrails. As we drove higher and higher, the vegetation diminished and the air got thinner. At 11,000 feet, we stopped by the tree line. This is the highest point in elevation at this latitude where trees can grow and is a boundary between sub-alpine forest and tundra. There is a stand of Bristlecone pine trees, which are among the oldest trees on the face of the earth, dating back over 1,700 years. Incredibly hard dense wood, they survive winter winds over 200 miles per hour by twisting but rarely breaking. As we ascended toward the peak, through alpine tundra vegetation, we drove slowly through a herd of mountain goats while our guests took pictures. From the peak parking lot, we hiked the steep 1/4 mile to the summit. Working for a major international airline, these folks had been all around the world, but never before on top of it. Yet there they were, people from the flat lands, standing at 14,264 feet above sea level. Here they had a 360 degree view of the world, hundreds of miles in all directions. Crawling out and laying flat on the edge of huge boulders, they could peak over the edge and peer down over 1,000 feet to the rocks below. After the summit pictures were taken, we hiked back down to the picnic area (a lowly 14,000 feet) and pulled out a cooler and toasted the top of the world with ice cold Coors. (Could it be any more Colorado?)

We headed back down the mountain to Evergreen and The Little Bear Saloon, for pizza, conversation, and certainly more Coors. The Little Bear was a famous mountain saloon, known throughout the country. It was an experience that had been part of our town for years. The place had real character, it was dark, dingy, and smelled of stale beer. And it was always fun to watch the faces on newcomers as they stared at the assorted collection of bras hanging curiously from the rafters. Each bra held a story that most likely involved multiple shots of tequila. And one might also guess that the women who "donated" their bras may have awaken the following day wondering where that bra was.

Willie Nelson had a home in Evergreen as well as Austin, Texas and would drop by to jam with the local bands whenever he was in town. Luckily, another Texan, Delbert McClinton, was playing that night and chances were that Willie would be in later to hang out with us locals.

Before the band started playing, we finished our business day of soft negotiations by dropping our big close; we explained that one final condition of our agreement would be that they MUST come to our headquarters here in Evergreen for training and information updates no less than three times a year, rather than us going to St. Louis and New York. (We also hinted that they might want to bring their skis.) We ended the evening listening to a local band wail out tunes while Ben and I sat back and listened to our guests relive their mountain experiences.

The next morning we signed the agreement. We began plans for introducing LeisureLink through TWA's PARS reservation system. We put together a detailed plan of first promoting our service to the TWA marketing reps, and once they were on board, we would introduce LeisureLink to the TWA travel agents at their upcoming travel conventions. These were always held in rotten places like Hawaii, the Caribbean or on board cruise ships, so we naturally felt obligated to attend them all.

By the end of the year, we had contracts in hand with two large distribution sources, International Travel Partners and TWA, and properties throughout the Caribbean and the Rockies. Now it was time for me to head to the various Hawaiian Islands to make more presentations and begin building our third data base. Yeah, I know, more tough duty, but hey, I was dedicated.

What a rush! In our first year, we had survived an earthquake, accomplished our beginning goals, and were on target with our plan for growth. We were adding quality employees on a weekly basis, which meant that we were also adding overhead. We were still blowing through our own money at a rapid pace, but we were convinced that the nonstop outgoing cash flow was no big deal because it was the valuable seed capital that would allow us to grow an immensely successful company. From this strong foundation, we would take Global Group public the following spring and raise millions to further accelerate our growth. Soon, we would begin to reap the rewards of our endeavors. We were having the time of our lives and we were absolutely psyched! As the band Timbuk3 sang, *"The future's so bright, we gotta wear shades"*.

2

The Stock Play

The secret to success is not in knowing everything. The secret is in knowing what you *don't* know, and finding those who do.

Ben and I had both grown other successful companies in the past, but they were privately held. Going public is a whole different ballgame and we knew that we were way out of our league.

In January, 1986 we started interviewing different investment banking firms to start the tedious process of preparing to become a publicly held company and selling stock in Global Group. There are extremely strict rules and procedures that must be followed when you go "public". These rules and regulations are written and enforced by the Securities and Exchange Commission (SEC), and are designed specifically to protect investors from scams and misinformation. We thought we had good controls on our business but these regulations are much more in depth, and at times they seemed an almost crushing weight on novices like us.

In order to successfully take a company through an Initial Public Offering (IPO) you have to have something that investors can understand and want. We had to grow Global Group to the point of showing that our plan was sound, our product was real, and that we actually had a customer base that desired our product. We had to show some cash flow, and we had to convince potential investors that there was a very real possibility of solid growth and profits in the future. All they had to do was invest the capital that would allow us to explode in growing the company. The contracts that we had in place, along with testimonials from happy customers, helped show that we were for real.

After meeting with several firms, we selected Rocky Mountain Wall Street to represent us and embarked down the unknown road of "going public". We were very fortunate to work with two very professional members with the firm that were a tremendous help to us. Dave Dawson was the firm's attorney and specialized in stock offerings. He was all business, with a methodical thought process, but also a hidden quick sense of humor. Dave was at times amused by my total lack of understanding of the very serious legal implications to almost everything about SEC regulations. He was the perfect balance for my intuitive drive to "market" our deal with my typical cavalier attitude and gift of gab.

Ed Larson was the head stock analyst for the firm and highly respected throughout the industry. Ed was from, as he pronounced it "Chicawgo", and loved to talk about "stawk issues". Ed came to Colorado to go to the

University of Colorado and after a stint in Chicawgo, he made Colorado his home. In the middle of a serious and spirited discussion about our business plans, Ed would interrupt himself to mention a stat about CU football. It was rumored that Ed's wife went into labor for their third son during a CU football game and he convinced her to "keep her knees together" until the end of the game. O.K., I started that rumor. The truth is that they left at half time, and to this day, their son Brent hates CU football.

Both Dave and Ed were the best at their professions, yet down to earth guys with great senses of humor. I met a few credible stock brokers though our experience that that I could trust, but most people in the stock industry at that time were very self serving and went for the quick return above all else. But Dave and Ed were the kind of guys that Ben and I trusted from day one. If you looked up the word "integrity" in the dictionary, you could visualize their pictures as an example. I could trust them with my life or my wife. All four of us were family guys in our 30s with the same values, work ethic, and dedication.

They helped us along and prepared us for some shocks ahead. One of the biggest shocks that young companies have when preparing for an IPO are the costs involved. From the time you sign an agreement with a stock firm you start writing checks. We decided on a $3 million offering, and our stock would start out at $5 per share. Along the way we realized that in addition to all of out of pocket expenses, which seemed endless, that the fees and commission to the stock firm would actually leave us approximately $2.4 million.

The second shock is how much of your time is taken away from running your company. When you're trying to raise money through investors, you are always on call, and will have to drop everything to meet, talk, and cater to them. Most company owners think that they may need to spend maybe a maximum of 20% of their time on going public, when in reality it can easily take 75% of their time. Very often this is at a critical time of growth in your company when your business needs you. The time spent trying to raise money to help your company grow, may actually be impeding the company's growth. But this was tolerable to us because it wouldn't last long and we'd get our money and be on our way...or so we thought.

1986 was an absolutely terrible time to try to take any company public in Colorado. The state had become notoriously known as the home of "Penny Stock Scams". Stock firms would offer stock in companies at a penny or perhaps five cents per share, and when they went up to ten cents the investors made a lot of money. The trouble was that many of the companies were bogus and the stock deals were Ponzi Scams. One firm was even nicknamed "Blind 'em & Rob 'em". Many stock brokers in Denver and around Colorado were sent to jail, and their misdeeds poisoned the investment climate.

Ed explained that there were two kinds of public offerings: a "best efforts" offering and a "firm" offering. With a "best efforts" the stock firm attempts to raise the amount that we want, but basically they raise whatever they can. With a "firm" offering, the amount is set and must be committed to by stock companies who agree to buy a portion of the deal before we would go public. We opted for a firm offering, because even though it might take a bit more time and effort, the money would be guaranteed. In this poor investment climate, a best effort could equate to very little.

After months of accounting reviews and regulatory preparations, we were ready to introduce our "deal" to the stock community. This should be easy. We'd do a few presentations and firms would make a commitment for our firm offering. We should have the whole thing wrapped up in thirty to forty five days.

3

Doin' The Due Dilly

T h,e stock gurus, attorneys, and accountants got busy with all of the legalities and started to prepare us for our big "Due Diligence" presentation, or the "Due Dilly" as they called it. A strange term to us common folk, this means that you get in front of all the stock brokers you can get together and try to convince them that they should want to invest their own, and their clients' money in your deal.

But this type of presentation was quite unlike the pure marketing and sales presentations that I had been doing successfully since I was in my twenties. Because of the SEC rules, the presentation becomes the original "no spin" zone. That is, it's not an advertisement but an explanation of what you're doing...backed up by real facts. You explain the market but must address all hidden risks along with the logical plan for the future, without making any pie-in-the-sky projections. And unlike the typical seminar format that I was used to, this was a seminar that could turn into an inquisition of questioning for more facts about what you would be doing with the money that investors might give you.

I must confess that, in years previous, I had

occasionally been successful by "tap dancing" my way through a sales presentation. A Due Diligence format is the best teaching method for anyone in sales and marketing because it makes you so much better by blending your presentation skills with good old fashion strict honesty. Dave enjoyed my positive attitude and sense of humor, but the disciplined SEC lawyer in him walked me through my presentation to make sure that my strong style would have none of my "blatant spin" (his term, not mine) that could damage our efforts.

Most "Due Dillys" were very dry and mostly boring. My challenge was to get in all the pertinent facts, but still make it enjoyable, and hopefully even a little fun.

Ed and his group at Rocky Mountain Wall Street got busy promoting our stock offering and the upcoming Due Diligence presentation. It would be at the Marriott Hotel, in a room that would hold 250. Ben and I were excited, because we knew that if they could fill the room, we could sell our deal. This was going to be fun.

Ed worked his network nonstop and we had RSVPs for 250, unheard of in this poor market. The big night came and we had a standing room only crowd of close to 300 stock brokers.

I was totally psyched. I had been doing seminars for years and loved being in front of audiences, the larger the better. At one stretch with our previous company, I had done over 70 seminars in 63 cities in 42 weeks and enjoyed every one. But this could be the biggest presentation of our professional lives and I practiced, drilled and rehearsed. This was before laptops and PowerPoint, so I had carefully created each slide with our graphics designer to have the strongest visual impact in a large room.

Ben was a master at putting together financial plans and could negotiate a great business deal with anyone. While I just watched in awe, it was Ben who sat with the President and the Board of Directors of a major airline and single handedly convinced them they should buy our previous little company for a basket full of cash. He was a corporate visionary with a dead serious business sense, yet a keen sense of humor, and could communicate with anyone on a one to one or a small group basis.

There was only one thing that I had forgotten.

Although he would never admit it, Ben was terrified of standing up and speaking in front of a large group of people.

Ed started off the presentation by going over financial information and built up to a positive introduction of Ben. After a polite amount of applause, Ben stood in front of this full room and began to freeze and stammer. It was like watching your ten year old daughter fall down during her ballet recital, you hurt more that she does. Ben pushed sluggishly through his opening remarks, forgetting many significant points as I watched the pained look on the faces of those that knew him and what he was capable of. He finally got to my introduction by saying, "Uh, I'm going to, uh, bring Steve out now. Steve is, uh, our Executive Vice President and uh, runs our sales and marketing. Steve and I came out here together from the Midwest to build our first company, and, uh, (laughing nervously) uh, we lived together by Cheesman Park for about six months. And we've been a team ever since. Here's Steve."

I stared at Ben as I passed him on the stage and was thinking furiously on the fly how to get things back on track. It was nice that Ben explained that we had been together through our other company and that we were a good team. Why he even mentioned where we had lived was really off the wall. See, as everyone in the audience knew, the Cheesman Park area of Denver is one of the strongest gay neighborhoods in the United States (as Seinfeld would say, "Not that there's anything wrong with that"). And like Seinfeld, I couldn't care less, but in 1986, Denver stock brokers were pretty much a homophobic group, and we were attempting to make a strong positive first impression on them.

"Thanks, Ben," I said as I pried the microphone from his frozen hand. "And thank all of you for joining us here this evening to hear our story and invest in our future. But before I get to the formal presentation about Global Group, I'd like to cover a couple of things. First, as Ben mentioned, we did live together in an apartment by Cheesman Park, but I'd also like to point out that we were rooming together only until we could move our lovely female wives of many years, and I might add with lovely breasts, and our families out here to Colorado."

The audience roared with laughter and applause, and I knew we had them back.

"Now that we have reestablished our fragile manhood, I'd like to point out one more thing. Dave, please stand up and give everyone a wave." Dave was surprised, but followed my direction. "This is Mr. Dave Dawson," I went on, "Dave is assisting us as an expert SEC attorney for Rocky Mountain Wall Street, and he's sitting here on the front row for a reason. You see, I've been doing major presentations for years, but I've gotta to tell you, this industry of yours is weird. You've got all of these rules about real facts, and no revenue projections.

That being said, Dave is afraid that I might revert to my pure marketing and sales persona. So if I stop, dead in my tracks in the middle of a sentence, it's because Dave has crossed his arms as a no-no signal."

Again, laughter and comforting applause. They were not only back, they were on our side.

Now for the closer. I flipped on the first giant slide. It was an almost three dimensional graphic in bold colors that simply screamed "$280 BILLION".

"Oh, WOW!" I exclaimed, "I just noticed that Dave has his arms, his legs, and his eyes crossed! I guess that I should point out that this $280 BILLION slide is NOT a projection of what I think our sales will be next year."

They were now howling with laughter. The

opening really got their attention, and from then on they listened intently. We all felt that the rest of the evening was a success. After the presentation was over, Ben stood with a drink in his hand and a smile on his face, laughing about his Cheesman Park statement, and answering anyone's questions. Off the demon stage and back to a one-on-one reality, he was once again the visionary that could sell our deal.

How could these people not want to invest in us?

4

On The Road Again

Two weeks later, Ed handed us another shocker. He told us that the feedback from the Due Dilly was great, but because of the increasingly sour climate in Colorado that our public offering would not be effective. The market in Colorado had a penny stock market mentality and a "real" offering wouldn't fly. We simply could not get our IPO completed at $5 per share unless we took the deal out of Colorado. We would have to try to syndicate it across the country through other firms. When this step was nearly complete, then we would meet again with the stock brokers in Denver to finish the offering.

That was just what Ben and I wanted to hear...more time, more money. We sat in silence for a moment and Ben said, "Hell, I was hoping to find some way to spend *all* of our money!" We started laughing and I started singing "On the road again" and we took Ed out to plan our road trips over some beers. We knew there was no turning back now.

So once again, we hit the road, only this time I was talking to stock companies instead of resorts. We knew that we were going to face stiff competition throughout the country. We had to convince firms that had never heard of us or our story to invest in us instead of their own deals that they were pushing. Our plan was simple. This was a numbers game. We'll keep meeting and meeting until we get the $3 million committed. I mean, please…it's only a piddly $3 million. Ben and Dave headed to the northeast while Ed and I headed to Florida. I've found that one of the best ways to really get to know someone is to go on a road trip together.

Ed and I spent our first long two weeks on Florida's east coast, ripe with small, but very wealthy investment firms. We covered Miami, Ft. Lauderdale, Pompano Beach and Boca Raton. We preset appointments and met with several influential stock firms every day, wining and dining the principals and then pitching our deal with their stock brokers during "lunch and learns." We were dropping money every day, hoping someone would agree to take a portion of the stock offering.

We ran into plenty of other stock deals to compete with and ours was from Colorado, the land of penny stock scams. Many of the firms were polite, but noncommittal. Others "loved our story and would work on it."

After thirteen days up and down the coast, and countless "Love it guys, it's a sure winner…but call us when you have others in the deal", we ended up in Pompano Beach for what we thought was a solid appointment with the owner of a strong regional stock firm. We sat in the reception area nervously for one hour before being told that the "gentleman" was not coming back to the office after lunch to meet with us because he had forgotten that he had a round of golf scheduled. His assistant asked that we leave our information and he would look at it later. That did it. I looked at Ed and said, "That's it, my friend, let's go find a medicinal beer."

We jumped into our 190 degree rental car and started driving down the coast. Around 3:00 pm, Ed spotted this little Oceanside restaurant and bar called the Whale's Spout on A1A, with a great deck facing the Atlantic. We went upstairs and outside to the large deck that hung over the beach, with soothing waves lapping beneath.

Yes, the day had been a total waste as far as getting investors, but let's look on the bright side to life…we're two guys from Colorado and for the first time in two weeks of being on the Florida coast, we are actually sitting in front of the ocean, at happy hour twofers time, and they actually had ice cold Coors. Could it get any better? Well yes it could. I still had some credit left on my credit cards.

So we sat outside in the breeze in our three piece pinstripe stockbroker monkey suits and chatted with the locals, listening to Jimmy Buffet tunes and ordering twofers by the twofers. Ah, the breeze was warm, the beer ice cold, and we got casual by peeling off our coats, vests and ties. We sat on the edge of the deck with our feet on the rails, planning our next day's attack with a beer in each hand. We didn't even notice the clouds approaching from the Atlantic.

Our waitress was Shirley, a friendly very tan, large woman with bleached hair and flesh-toned teeth. She had brought us several beers and was back to take our "same thing?" order. As she leaned over and exposed a very unattractive biker tattoo above her right breast, she said, "Hey y'all, I don't know if you noticed, but everyone else has left the deck because of that bigass squall heading this way."

Ed and I looked at the clouds, from the tip of the ocean, up to…well, as far up as we could see and yes, they were getting really dark. We just laughed and Ed said, "Thanks for the info, but those aren't really dark clouds so there's no rain out there. And if there is rain, I'm sure it'll blow right over. Steve and I'll ride it out right here. Two more twofers please."

A few minutes later she brought out the beers and informed us that she had just finished shutting all of the window shutters. It was her bet was that we would get blasted in ten minutes. Once again, Ed and I looked at each other, and laughed.

"Look honey," I said, through my Coors-found wisdom, "We've been fighting our own storms all week and those bastards can't defeat us, so a little shower won't either."

"*Whatever*, big boys, but I'm goin' in, and we have to lock the shutters on the door from the inside. So if y'all are stayin' out, you ain't comin' in. Hopefully we'll see y'all in about a half hour."

The wind against our faces got stronger and stronger, but it was warm and felt wonderful. That was followed by a mist that was even better. Within about three minutes, however, the mist quickly switched to the level of a car wash. I could see the locals peeking through the shutters, toasting us and laughing hysterically!

Trapped outside, Ed and I glanced at each other, and leaned forward against the railing, into the wind and horizontal rain, grasping a Coors bottle in each hand as if they were ski poles. We screamed and laughed as we pretended we were downhill skiing back in Colorado. As we were getting totally blasted by the warm fierce deluge, we yelled to the wind and the world, "We've got the right deal, and you bastards cannot and will not defeat us!"

After the storm blew through, the manager opened the shutters and the door and handed us both two beers saying, "Here ya'll go, guys, this round, and a cab ride is on me." We took a bow as the laughing locals came out to applaud us. We spent the next few hours dying out and eating shrimp and grouper with the locals. Our pinstripe suits were never the same, but Ed and I have been best friends for life.

☆☆☆☆☆☆☆☆☆☆

Ben, Dave, Ed and I spent almost two months on the road, east coast, west coast, even Ed's Chicawgo, making presentations to over 40 companies, while still trying to effectively run our company from afar. When we got back to Colorado we had more meetings and presentations with prospects that would fly in to see our operation.

One such prospective investor was Hal Stewart. Hal ran a large fund in Seattle. He had once been a successful professional baseball player and though he was now 70, was still quite fit. He came across as a good 'o boy, but he was as sharp as they come. He spent a day and a half with us, going over our operations and meeting our employees, who now numbered twelve. Over dinner, Hal asked Ben and me the strangest question. "Boys, when was the last time you failed real big?"

Ben and I gave each other a bit of a startled look and I replied, "Excuse me sir?" Ben chucked and said, "We haven't and we certainly don't intend to start now. We have a sound plan and it doesn't include failure. Why do you ask?"

"Oh, because you will," replied Hal. "It's not a matter of if, only when. I was just hoping that you had already gotten it out of the way."

We gave a quick glance to each other and passed on Hal's strange remark. We instead steered the conversation on how successful we had been in building previous companies. As we ate dinner, we nonchalantly intertwined how we both grew up in farm towns and started working at an early age, and how we had been raised with a good old fashion Midwestern work ethic. The other little fact that Ben had gone to college on a baseball scholarship didn't hurt.

As we were sipping our after dinner drinks, Hal gave us the news. "Well, boys, I'm going to invest in you. I don't bet on the horses, I bet on the jockeys, and I think you two have the determination and persistence to ride anything across the finish line."

"Thank you, sir," Ben said. "You won't be disappointed."

So far, we had commitments from 28 firms to take anywhere from 10,000 to 20,000 shares each. Hal's investment put us over the top, and finally, on June 4, 1986, we "went public" with a firm $3 million offering. After expenses, we put $2.4 million in the bank. Now we were finally off to the races.

5

Now What?

After a big celebration party with our employees and their families, and a few good nights sleep at home, we settled back into the management mode for the next chapter of our growth. First, we finally were able to sign the lease for the new office building that we had found months before. We were splitting at the seams and were more than ready to move. And secondly it was finally time to kick in our hiring plan to start bringing on more high quality people.

Because we were exploding in our growth, we wanted strong entrepreneurial spirits. We had a two part formula for finding the best people for every position. The first part, naturally, was the strong core capabilities to perform the required and requested tasks. But just as important to us was the second part, which was strength and quality of character.

After it was determined that a person had the skills we were looking for, we conducted a final interview to look for the quality character traits that would fit our goals and the company personality for the team that we were building. These were people who had accepted risks and paid the price to reach their goals. They were quick thinkers with an insatiable appetite to learn and grow. They were competitive, and had the drive to strive and win in whatever they were doing. They could follow the company plan, but had the ability to take charge when needed. Every single person that we added to our growing team had the ability to become a leader in their department and grow within the company. And, above all, they were honest and had a high degree of integrity. We knew that together, capabilities and character would create an unstoppable force.

We strived to find the finest people possible and believed that, no matter what kind of company or industry that we might be in, the greatest asset that we could ever have was the people on our team, and we were dedicated to treating our employees the best that we possibly could. Besides the standard benefits, we budgeted for important things that would bond everyone and make growing together more fun. This included parties, cookouts, Colorado skiing, whitewater rafting, company softball, and family events. We were building a company family. We were all in this together and worked to keep it that way.

Speaking of families, for the first time in 18 months, Ben and I actually took a salary, and our families actually had health insurance. Our salaries were no big deal, because we wanted to show investors that we were in no way greedy. The only "perk" that we took was a monthly allowance for company cars. We both got our well deserved luxury sports sedans, which we naturally "needed" to shuffle investors and customers around.

It was an incredibly wonderful feeling to know how proud my family was of me. My wife, Laura, and our son, and daughter had been supportive of this crazy entrepreneur and now it was time to start paying them back. I said that I was doing all this for them. The deep down selfish truth was that I was doing it for me. This was the greatest high that I could ever imagine and it was the most addictive thrill that I had ever experienced. Ben and I were on the fast track and so far it was a speeding adrenaline induced roller coaster power trip, and we were in the front car and in control. Our plan was working and we were on our way to amassing an incredible amount of personal wealth.

Oh, this was going to be fun.

6

The Surprise Addition

Although one of our top priorities was still promoting our stock and watching it grow, we had to get back to our core business. While I was planning my next trips to keep building LeisureLink's growing database of resorts, Ben headed to Kansas to meet with International Travel Partners (ITP) for an update meeting on our preferred supplier agreement.

After Ben's meeting, he called me from the airport to ask, "So, Steve, how would you like to own a travel agency franchise company?"

"Say what?" I replied. "What's up, what have you been drinking?"

Ben started laughing and said, "Nothing yet, but I'll be back to the office in a couple of hours, so ice down the beer. partner, cause our little ol' company is about to get a whole lot bigger!" And with a huge laugh, he hung up on me.

Ben left me hanging on his words about what could be happening with ITP. I tried to get back to what I had been doing but this new tease consumed me. I thought that I knew what he was inferring but I had to wait for him to get back and confirm it. At 8:00 pm Ben walked into the office with a Cheshire grin on his face and a thirst for a cold beer.

Ben popped the top on a Coors and exclaimed, "Well, let's get down to planning our next new company!"

For the next three hours we plotted what our new corporate directions could be – taking over International Travel Partners. Having gone through the earthquake adventure with the principals of ITP, we had built a strong trusting relationship, and had gotten to know them quite well. As we were working side by side with them to strengthen our program, they began to discuss their inner workings with us and even asked our advice on how they could improve their business growth. Through our meetings, we realized that they were at the point in their corporate life that many companies go through. They were at a maturation point where their growth was stagnating. They had run out of fresh ideas, and basically were in a rut. We also discovered that they were running short on operating cash.

We knew their business inside out because we had been working with them for four years as a preferred supplier through Global, as well as our previous company. The question was, did we want to make a huge jump into the travel agency franchise business on top of being a travel industry software company only one month after going public? Growing up in Indiana, we had a saying, "You can't run with the big dogs by lying on the porch." Ben and I didn't just want to run with the big dogs, we wanted to be the lead dog, so the answer was a resounding YES!

Combining our technological expertise and knowledge of the travel industry with ITP' experience in franchising, we would create the strongest travel company in existence. We agreed that this was a once in a lifetime shot to get huge with a known entity, and we were not going to be denied. We just had to figure out how to make the deal work.

We brought in Dave and Ed and our attorneys and accountants to study the possible ways to finance the acquisition. We considered what positive and negative effects it might have on our stock, both in the short and long term. We met for days. While these very talented numbers, legal, and investment minds were plotting the plan for a major corporate acquisition, I was sitting in the conference room with my marketing mind spinning at warp speed, thinking how I was going to create national press coverage and push our stock price up. I knew our team could figure a way to make this work and I was plotting how to double the revenues of ITP when they became part of Global Group (and you thought our name was presumptuous).

Three days and many conference calls later, we had the rough draft of the agreement and three weeks later we had a signed deal. We would make a large down payment and complete the purchase over the next two years.

It was time for another big celebration party. International Travel Partners was now a wholly owned subsidiary of Global Group. We made the announcement to the press and our stock went up 30%.

In a little over a month since we went public, we had two companies. We toasted our employees, "Look out world, there's a new big dog on the block!" Here we were, two guys in our thirties, grabbing the world by the neck. If we weren't yet invincible, we were certainly unstoppable. Yes, for the time being we were pretty full of ourselves.

Now it was time for another regrouping. We would need even more office space to accommodate our new ITP employees. We went back to our building management company and renegotiated options to take over the entire building if needed. Our office building sat outside of our beautiful little mountain town of Evergreen. The west side of our building looked out over the mountains, while from the east side we had views of the Denver skyline. Less than a quarter of a mile from the building was the largest buffalo herd reserve in the west, and we had free roaming herds of deer and elk that would come by and stare into our windows.

We immediately began the transitional planning for the blending of our teams. We brought in the key people from ITP and got to work on how soon we could get them and their families moved. It was not a tough sell, asking people if they wanted to move from Kansas to Evergreen, Colorado.

We also got to work on a new program to increase revenues. ITP had 230 travel agency franchises but most were small "Mom & Pop" locations, each doing only about $1 million a year in sales. Travel agencies made an average of 10% commission on all travel they sold. ITP corporate made money from franchise fees from the agencies, plus a piece of the commissions negotiated on behalf of their agencies. We wanted to get much bigger agencies on board because the real money would come from override commissions paid to us by the major airlines, cruise lines, and resorts for increasing their sales. To do this, we introduced a new ITP Affiliate Program. We targeted larger companies who would become affiliates of ITP for a fee of $5,000 to $10,000. As such, they would be paid higher commissions for the travel that they sold. In a few months time, we had grown to nearly 300 agencies that had annual revenues in excess of $500 million, and we had bargaining strength with all of the major travel companies. We were able to actually create a shift in a carrier's business by having our agencies sell to or away from that particular carrier. In return for our support, we negotiated commissions of upwards of 20%, depending on the industry, hotels, cruise lines, airlines, etc. This quickly became a win-win situation for everyone. For example, our agencies that were making 10% from an airline, would now be paid 13% - a 30% increase, and we would be paid 2% for a total of 15% from the carrier, and the carrier gained a loyal sales force to increase their sales. We were very quickly becoming one of the largest and strongest distributors of travel products in the world. The press loved our story and the investment community loved our progress. Our stock was rising.

But we wanted more.

We were now on a new quest, no it was going to be a crusade! We knew that there were new ways to sell travel that no one had yet thought of, and we were committed to an unrelenting mission to discover them all and discover them first. We had meetings with industry people and then all of our employees for ideas. These were fun put and take sessions where anyone could throw something out and see what might stick. Some ideas seemed really off the wall, some just silly, and some that sounded crazy, but we kept going until things emerged that actually made sense.

And anyway, what, exactly is a crazy idea? Just six months before, the crazy idea that two guys working on a software idea would now have 300 travel agencies doing $500 million in revenues would have brought on hysterical laughter. Two major ideas came from these meetings and our newest team members from the travel industry. Both were going to make us all very wealthy.

7

Attention Shoppers

ITP had discovered that Kmart was looking at new areas to increase their business. With over 2,100 stores and approximately $22 billion in annual sales, Kmart was, at the time, the second largest retailer in America. They were the powerhouse that we were looking for to create a whole new method of sales and distribution for our new travel products. We set the meeting and pitched them our new business proposal.

We would develop private labeled travel packages for Kmart. These would include such things as Caribbean cruises, three day Bahamian getaways, and Colorado ski trips. Kmart would advertise the packages in their Sunday newspaper supplements with an 800 number to call. The 800 number would be our new reservation center, where we would handle all calls and book all travel on their behalf. Kmart would pay only for the placement of the ads. All other costs involved for the development of the packages, of building the reservation center, and all administration of the programs would be paid totally by us. Why would we agree to do that?

Because we also had one big stipulation. After

we proved to Kmart that the program was a success, they would agree to invest a minimum of $3 million in Global. We did this for three big reasons. First, we were blowing through money at a very rapid pace. Second, we knew that the news would pump up our stock. Third, and most importantly, we were creating a new suitor. One of our original goals was to build the company to make it attractive to a large suitor and sell it off. A $3 million investment could make Kmart commit to us, and would also make us more attractive to other potential suitors.

We submitted our proposal to Kmart's powers that be, and it was accepted one week later. We got busy on our newest project, preparing to launch in the first quarter of 1987. One more unbelievable chapter was about to begin.

We realized that there were even greater margins in creating our own travel packages and selling them through Kmart, as well as our 300 travel agencies. We also knew that the only way to be in total control of distributing our own travel products was to have our own reservation center. We quickly set out to build the most technologically sophisticated reservation center there could be. We brought in design experts to create a raised floor plan that would house all of the computer cabling beneath the floor and a separate air conditioning room for the computer that would be the brains of the system. We took over the first floor of our building. The walls had to go for the new center so we decided to get a head start on the construction crew with an employee "knock down the walls" after work party. Ah, what better bonding for our team than a good old fashion barn raising in reverse. Pizza, beer, and sledge hammers. Laughing and cheering, we were symbolically knocking down any and all obstacles to our company's success. It was a fun night that got everyone excited about the future, which was getting brighter and brighter every day.

While construction began, we began assembling a whole new team of experts. This time, we went after, and got the best from the airline and cruise line reservation centers. We started looking for the experts in the industry that we could hire that could initiate our new programs. These were professionals that knew how to build a call center and how to run it. We also brought in experienced travel professionals that knew how to work with the various vendors to build and price vacation packages. These newest team members gave up some very good benefits to join us to start something new and exciting, and in return they became part of a team who appreciated their talent, ideas, and input. Instead of the typical dark cramped quarters they were used to, we designed a bright, spacious, comfortable reservation center with great views. Gee, what a strange concept, creating a place where people actually want to come to work.

Another powerful addition that we were able to pull off was to hire Dave away from Rocky Mountain Wall Street to become our COO and corporate counsel. Unfortunately, Ed left Rocky Mountain Wall Street for a better position in Seattle. We would miss him and his talent.

We kept adding the best management people we could find, and they in turn were building their own specific teams. Many of these professionals had come from bigger companies with bigger titles. We wanted and needed their skills, but we also wanted down-to-earth people.

We had a sign that read "Please Leave Egos At The Door". It was our polite way of reminding everyone, "You're very smart and talented and powerful, so welcome to our team. To be an effective part of our company, know yourself, believe in yourself, trust in yourself, then get over yourself." Each person had their own area of expertise, but we stressed the analogy that once the chess game is over, the pawns and the king go back into the same box.

We strongly believed that every person that joined us had the potential for leadership, and we would help them develop it. We strived for and succeeded in assembling a fantastic group of positive personalities that shared ideas and mutual respect. Our common goal was to build a company unlike any other, have fun doing it, and all would reap the future rewards.

It was uplifting to finally have actual departments with real live managers, because when you first start a company you use what I termed "Hat Rack Management". That is, Ben and I wore the necessary hat that was needed, i.e. manager, sales, accounting, marketing, HR, fireman, etc.

All of our new department managers were going through their own trials by fire, even as they were getting settled in. We created our executive committee (EXCOM) and it seemed that we were constantly in short "think-plan-do" sessions, followed by companywide meetings to keep everyone in the loop. We were master jugglers, and boy, did we have a lot of balls in the air.

So why not one more big one?

Floating A New Idea

Cruise lines were going through enormous growth and change in the mid 80s. They were once thought of as stuffy old boats with stuffy old people, but with cruise lines like Carnival, this was changing fast. New ships were being added quickly and they were bigger, brighter, roomier, and best of all, they were now really fun.

Cruise lines also had higher margins and paid higher commissions than traditional travel vendors. We were working with all the major cruise lines to put together vacation packages for our travel agencies and the Kmart program through our new reservation center, utilizing our LeisureLink software, when we decided that the cruise industry was strong enough to merit a whole new franchise company.

Building a new franchise business meant developing a new corporate division with a new team of people. Paramount in our hiring search was finding the top people in the cruise industry. We were very fortunate to hire Bill Lever. As a Senior VP of a major cruise line, Bill was the consummate pro. He was an expert in the cruise industry and a very valuable asset to any company. He was given free reign to create the business plan for CRUISE AWEIGH, our new cruise-only franchise company. The stores would be designed to look like the inside of a ship, and we would sell cruises, cruises and more cruises. Consumers would visit the stores for cruise seminars and visit with cruise representatives to learn what great vacations we could offer. We projected that each new franchise would produce approximately $5 million in first year revenues. We would first offer territories to our existing travel agency owners, and then sell franchises to the general public. We would open our first prototype in the second quarter of 1987 and our goal was 30 locations in 1987 and 50 more in 1998.

Within thirty days, Bill brought together top talent from several cruise lines to join him for our newest division. They were a blend of talented people, young and old, and they immediately understood that they were part of not just a new cruise business, but part of the multifaceted team. As such, their time and duties would be dispersed to various projects as needed.

For the first time in our rapid, explosive growth, we had a new member of our team that I simply did not like. Bill hired Stan Radtke, a national sales manager from a large cruise line. He knew the industry inside and out. He was a tall, good looking tan guy who was perfectly dressed. I had an intuitive knack for knowing personalities and this guy just didn't seem real. He came across as very personable, maybe too much so, maybe too patronizing. I couldn't figure out what it was about Stan, but something just didn't seem to fit.

I mentioned my impression to Ben and he dismissed it. "Yeah, he's got a line of B.S., but so do you. Did it occur to you that maybe his personality is too much like yours and there's a little mental competition going on?" Ben asked.

"Hmm, that one cut", I replied. "You might be right, but I've gotta tell you, Ben, if B.S. made music, this guy would be a brass band."

I thought about Ben's statement for a few days, and decided that maybe he was right. I would just leave it alone and it would probably work itself out. Stan was reporting directly to Bill, and I wouldn't spend that much time with him. I would find out if he was a team player during our EXCOM meetings. Later, I learned that my instincts were right.

It was now October, five short months since we had gone public. And gee, all we had to show for it was an innovative leisure travel system called LeisureLink with a contract to sell it through a major airline, 300 travel agency franchises doing $500 million in sales, and the largest and most sophisticated computerized reservation center in the United States. Oh yeah, we also had a contract with the second largest retailer in the world to develop programs for them and then have them invest in us, and we were working on getting ready to launch our brand new cruise-only franchise company.

We were simultaneously balancing all projects

while constantly promoting our stock and our progress to the investment community. They liked what they heard because our stock had doubled.

We were now had over 80 great employees and had taken over 90% of our building. We were constantly having visitors, including existing and potential investors, franchisees, travel industry executives, family members, and the press.

One of the most rewarding things to me was that, time and time again, visitors told us that they could actually feel the positive energy when they came into our building. None of us were surprised because we not only felt it, we lived off of it. We were this energy charged group of people that loved life and what we were doing in it. Everyone was a pro who was very serious about doing their best job possible, and we were also very serious about having a fun time doing it. Spontaneous hugs and horseplay were part of our corporate personality. We had a work hard – play hard, philosophy and we probably laughed together, and enjoyed each other's company more than any company out there.

We settled into the last part of the year in a bit of a routine, for once just trying to manage existing things instead of creating new ones. We worked diligently on each program, defining and refining plans and procedures, while placing the right players into the programs best suited to their talents.

We ended the year with a big family holiday

party. As a thank you to the families, we took over a hotel with great kid amenities and made it an overnight party for all. We grownups had a great holiday dinner with free flowing champagne, and year end toasts from everyone. We next had the holiday gift exchange. Everyone brought a wrapped gift with a maximum value of $25.00. As the MC, I went around the room and picked the order of the people who would come to the gift table and choose the package of their choice and open it in front of the audience. There were some very funny off color gag gifts that got crazy, and people were laughing themselves into tears. After our dinner party was complete, we danced and partied the night away, while the kids partied their night into morning with chaperoned fun at the pool and arcade.

It was a wonderful end to a wonderful year. As we were all finally saying good night, I wondered what the New Year would bring.

Could this thing keep getting better?

What, No Centerfold?

By the end of January, 1987, we were getting all the pieces put together to announce the start of the Kmart vacation program. We decided that we would do a trial ad in one city to test the response capabilities of our new reservation center. The center was doing a good job of handling calls and bookings from our agencies, but we were unsure about a potential massive call volume. We worked out the final programs while Kmart started to design the ad campaign and decide on the test market. We would roll out the first test in late February. This, along with all of our other projects should be enough to keep us quite busy, right?

Not quite.

One evening, after so-called work hours and over pizza and beers, we were having a full EXCOM meeting. It was rare to get all of our executive committee members together at one time because each member was leading a particular project and we were always coming and going like ships passing in the night. After updates from all, we started playing "put and take, what if, and see what sticks". We were kicking around new ways to promote and sell travel programs.

One of our travel experts came up with the idea of a travel magazine. At the time there were no pure travel magazines in print. The thoughts began to fly around the room.

What if we would start our own travel magazine?

What should we call it?

What if it was a high gloss, first class magazine that would tell stories of great destinations with glorious pictures?

Couldn't all of the destinations be visited through our vacation packages, which could be purchased by calling our agencies or our 800 number at our new reservation center?

And how about travel tips?

Hey, how about a centerfold? O.K., maybe not.

Why not build our own travel club with the magazine?

We could offer ads exclusively to our travel vendor partners.

This thing could actually pay for itself, hell, it could actually make money.

The ideas bounced off the walls like racquet balls for hours. One wall in the conference room was all dry wipe board, and we would jump up and write down a new thought, which would lead to the next.

Man, this was fun.

We could make this thing work and it would be the first travel magazine of its kind. "Just one little thing, gang", said Ben. "I hate to bring this up, but who knows anything about publishing a professional magazine?"

We all looked at each other and burst out laughing. Dave responded, "That's never stopped us before!"

"Look", I added, "One of our credos is that the secret to success isn't in knowing everything, it's knowing what we don't know and finding those who do. Well, we all agree that this can work, so tomorrow I'll get busy and find out who can make it happen." And with that, a new project was born. It would be named "LeisureLink, the world's leisure travel magazine".

The next morning, I got on the phone and started playing "six degrees of separation" with our business network. By the following day I started getting calls back with leads to professional publishing companies that came highly recommended. Our other projects were flowing smoothly with our new team leaders, so I was able to commit time to exploring our move into the world of magazine publishing.

After interviewing several publishing companies, we settled on Target Market Publications in Westport, Connecticut. We chose them because they impressed us with their professionalism, and they were a subsidiary of Marketing Corporation of America (MCA), who was a major marketing consulting firm. Together, they offered a one-two punch with great production and marketing ideas.

Ben and I flew out for two days of initial meetings. Their office setup in Westport was just about as desirable as ours in Evergreen. They had a beautiful Victorian home as a guest house for visitors, and their offices overlooked the Saugatuck river. After discussing our goals for the magazine, they assigned a team to us that would meet our needs and blend with our personalities.

Bill Redmond would lead the project and be working with me one on one to make me a "publisher". This project was bigger than I anticipated but it was a great learning experience. When I pick up a magazine now, I have profound respect for the detailed planning, organization, and dedicated time that goes into it.

We determined that we could publish the first issue by late summer, for about $180,000. We would have an initial run of 300,000 copies that would be distributed through our 300 travel agencies. We started working on editorial content, story ideas, publication size, and sources of advertising. We would limit our advertising to the vendors that we were already contracts with, which would strengthen our relationships and help us sell more of their products. We would bear the majority of the cost for the first issue, and our projections showed that we would break even on issue two, and actually turn a small profit by issue three. Profit would be nice, but the purpose of the magazine was to be a marketing and advertising tool to help us sell travel and build our credibility as the experts in the industry.

We wanted to have a good balance of travel tips, stories and destinations in each issue. From

Hawaii, to cruises, to Carnival in Rio, to Colorado skiing, we would have something for everyone.

Some of the stories about particular destinations might require me going to the destinations, but once again, I had to do what I had to do. I needed to "research" some new resorts in Hawaii for our first issue and I planned a working vacation. For the first time since we started the company, I was finally taking my wonderful family on the "thank you" vacation that they deserved. We started out on the Big Island and explored Kilauea, the active volcano. Next we stayed in Ka'anapali in exotic Maui and drove the famous road to Hana, stopping along the way to dive from the cliff's edge at the Seven Pools. We flew on to Poipu and were awed by the breath taking beauty of the island of Kauai. Snorkling in the crystal clear water of Poipu Bay, we came across what we all swore were plaid fish. Finally we spent a few days in O'ahu where we toured Pearl Harbor, and stayed on the North Shore where we attempted big time surfing. In all, we spent three weeks in gorgeous oceanfront condos on four incredible islands, and yes, I really did produce beautiful pictures and stories about the resorts. You know, I could really get to like this publishing business.

10

The Blue Light Panic

got back from Hawaii just in time for the launch of the first Kmart ad. The Detroit area was chosen for the first test market as it was close to Kmart headquarters in Troy, Michigan. The ad was placed in the center of their Sunday supplement, between kids' clothes and home and garden tools. It was a full page of trips to the Bahamas and a special cruise that we arranged. The ad had the 800 number of our reservation center. We were all waiting nervously for the results.

Would this work? Would anybody really pick up the phone and buy travel this way? Would Kmart be satisfied with the results?

By 9:00 a.m., Sunday morning, all our lines were full and they stayed full. We were selling travel packages as fast as our team could answer the calls. We were going to turn the world of selling travel upside down!

And then our immediate success sneaked up and smacked us right between the eyes and bloodied our noses. At 2:00 p.m. that Sunday, our state of the art computerized phone system froze. The shear volume of incoming calls shut down one of the most sophisticated systems in existence. The system was, however, able to track how many calls could NOT be answered, and by Monday morning we had over 3,000 unanswered calls.

Our first reaction was the cold sweating panic of crushing failure. We got in way over our heads. We were going to look like a bunch of amateur fools that don't know what we're doing. Kmart will hate us, drop the program and never invest a penny in us. Our investment in the reservation center would never be recouped. Our competitors would be laughing at us. Our stock would drop. Our employees would lose faith in us. Our wives, kids, and even our dogs would hate us.

It was time for an emergency damage control strategy session to plan our proactive call to Kmart the first thing Monday morning. We went outside for fresh air and hopefully a fresh outlook. We sat outside in our picnic area and looked at the mountains, took a few slow, very deep breaths, and started searching for the silver lining.

There were several positives that we could justify. One, this was a test. Two, the response was literally an overwhelming success. Three, our system could be tweaked to handle greater volume, and four, we just proved that Kmart could sell travel, a lot of travel.

Monday morning, we made the call to Kmart and much to our great relief and delight, Kmart agreed with our assessment. It was time for a quick time out to regroup and reorganize our game plan. The second test was postponed for

30 days and we now knew what to expect and would be ready for it. We would make this wildly successful and Kmart would follow through with their investment in us. We had dodged the bullet, (bullet hell, it was a missile) and now we would not be denied. Thirty days later the second ad ran and it was an absolute success! In four days we booked over $400,000 in vacation packages. Kmart was very pleased with the result. We had just gotten back on the fast track to greater success.

11

Rabbit Out Of A Hat?

The other areas and programs were flowing smoothly, and our continual press releases and promoting kept our stock climbing. It was now April and our stock was at $10.00, up from our original $5.00 in less than ten months.

We were still in the planning phase of LeisureLink, the magazine, and I had a meeting scheduled with Bill Redman to review our progress. Bill called to tell me that he was going to be in Chicago with another client and asked if I could meet him there.

He would be staying at the grand old Drake hotel. I had always loved this place. My mom and dad used to stay there when I was a kid growing up in Indiana. They'd bring back the little bars of soap, which my older brother and I used to soap the neighbors' windows at Halloween. But I digress.

Bill asked me to meet him in the bar at 6:00 p.m. The Cog d'Or bar was a classic in Chicago. It was warm, with dark cherry wood paneling and red leather seats. It was the kind of place where you'd expect Frank Sinatra to stroll in with Dean Martin, and you felt like you had to order a Manhattan. But I was from Colorado and ordered a Coors. They didn't have Coors, so when in Rome, I ordered a Manhattan, and requested Sinatra tunes.

I was enjoying my drink and humming along to "That's life", when Bill came in. He looked tired but excited. He had just finished the first of a two day marketing strategy meeting with his largest client.

"My client has come through some tough financial times and are turning things around", explained Bill. "We just spent the entire day looking at new ways to maximize the company's reputation and image to spin off new areas of business."

"Who's the client?" I asked.

Bill looked at me and smiled, "I think you may have heard of them, Playboy Enterprises."

"Heard of them?" I replied, "I grew up on Playboy! I still have my Playboy Club Keycard. I can see why you're excited."

Like many young men in the sixties and early seventies, Playboy was the guide to my future fantasy life. Growing up in Winchester, Indiana, I graduated from *Boys Life* magazine to *Playboy*, and it was this new found publication that was my link to the worldly sophistication that I, in my dreams, would one day achieve. To obtain this height of sophistication, I'll have you know that I did actually read the articles (as well as occasionally admiring the photo layouts of lovely women).

After a few titillating thoughts and teenage memories of stapled women and had passed, I regained reality as Bill discussed the fact that

Playboy was like any other large company with a product. They had to keep the product fresh, appealing and ahead of the competition, and they had to look for ways to increase distribution and sales. Since the first Playboy magazine was published in December 1953, the adult entertainment industry had gone through dramatic changes and evolutions. The magazine which was once the stand alone empire and professional standard of the industry now had many competitors that were trying to win on the sleaze factor. There was a cultural change going on that had a diluting effect of the company's growth.

In 1960, the first Playboy Club opened. Playboy Clubs grew coast to coast and became the most successful nightclub chain in history, selling more than 2.5 million membership keys. Once the absolute place for the "in" crowd, the clubs had run their course, and 1986 saw the closing of the last Playboy Club.

Playboy Enterprises, like so many companies in other industries, was at a cross road in their growth and direction for their future. Hugh Hefner's daughter Christie became the new President and Chief Operating Officer, and under her astute leadership, the company cut many of their losses, and was now back in a strong cash position. They were looking for ways to build new divisions and directions to capitalize on their core strengths.

Cable television was catching on, and the Playboy channel was already a hit. They were also entering the growing home video arena.

Playboy had two very positive things going for them that would help them create vertical marketing opportunities. The first was their logo. In the mid 80's the Playboy Rabbit Head was the second most recognized logo in the world, behind only Coca Cola.

Second, Playboy had built a huge subscriber data base over the years, and it was among the highest demographic and median income level of any magazine in any category. They also had the data base of former Playboy Club members, and they had created a "Playboy Preferred" list of the top 500,000 subscribers on a very high income demographic level.

As Bill was speaking, my mind was spinning like a top on steroids. "So, my consulting job is to help them find new areas for profitable growth", said Bill.

"Got any ideas?"

I thought I was going to explode. This gargantuan window of opportunity had just opened for Global, and I was about to blast through it.

"Do I have any ideas?" I answered, "You bet I have ideas, tons of ideas, hours of ideas. Not just ideas, great ideas! Not just ideas, but answers, solutions! Bill, this can be, no this IS the match made in heaven."

"Damn, Steve", joked Bill, "I was hoping you might show some enthusiasm. So what are these solutions?"

"Three words, Bill...Travel, Travel, Travel! We can make Travel work for Playboy, and make Playboy tons of money!"

Our minds were off and running. For the next four hours we sat there in that great old bar, blending ideas with the occasional Manhattan. While I babbled, Bill scribbled down notes on our drink napkins.

Global could sell Playboy Travel to, as we said in the industry, the masses and the asses.

We could develop private labeled adult vacation packages for Playboy at the finest upscale resorts. These would enhance their quality image and would come with high margins.

We'd also do less expensive packages for the masses.

We'd advertise and market through the magazine and the Playboy channel.

How about special Playboy Cruises?

I've got it, how about a Playboy Club Member Reunion Cruise, complete with Bunnies.

We'd offer monthly drawings for fabulous trips in PLAYBOY Magazine and on the cable channel.

Hey, why not a Playboy Travel Club?

We'd advertise and place articles in LeisureLink, the magazine.

As we continued, Bill quickly ran out of napkins and started writing on the white cotton table cloth. We started going over the possible numbers of trips and how much could be made. I explained for example that if only 5% of their

500,000 "preferred" list would book a Playboy theme cruise, it would equate to 25,000 cruise bookings. At an average price of $1,800 per cabin, it would be approximately $45 million in cruise sales alone.

I reminded Bill that as with Kmart, we would do all of the work and pay for the programs. Playboy would simply do the promotions. And we all will make a lot of money.

"Get us in there, Bill", I pleaded, "and I promise that I'll make you the star for finding us."

We finished about midnight and before we left, Bill paid the waiter $50 for the table cloth and folded it up. I think he still has it in a box somewhere.

Bill now had a new game plan for the next day's meeting – Playboy Travel.

As we were heading to our rooms, Bill called out, "Oh, Steve, about our meeting today to update you on LeisureLink, the Worlds Leisure Travel Magazine; we're on schedule and it's looking good."

That's the kind of update meeting I liked... short and to the point. And besides, all I could think of was our opportunity with Playboy Enterprises. This would be the rabbit out of the hat.

Bill called me two days later and toyed with me, "So when was the last time you were invited to the Playboy headquarters in Chicago? Christie Hefner and her team got excited with our ideas and would like you to come out next week. Can you make it?"

Yeah, that was a tough sell. "Gosh, Bill", I said, "You better give me a nanosecond to think about it – YES!"

The next week, I entered the corporate halls of Playboy. This was their original office and not what I had expected. It was rather dark, even a little dingy. But walking down the halls was like walking through a history museum, with some of the old famous Playboy art and artifacts on display. Bill and I waited in Christie Hefner's office and I was quite nervous. I didn't need to be.

Christie entered with her CFO and the president of their licensing division. I was immediately impressed by her professionalism. Christie was only 32 years old but was not only running the company, it was she who had turned it around.

She was friendly, unassuming and down to earth. I guess that I expected someone flamboyant and glamorous. She was very attractive, but in a wholesome Midwestern way, very little makeup or jewelry. She didn't need any.

She was all about business and proved instantly that she knew her stuff. She had already done her homework and knew just about everything about us. She loved our creativity, but fired off ten or twelve opening questions about our capabilities. Her questions were always polite, and always direct. One sensed that she was on a mission and that there was no time for idle chit chat and certainly not B.S.

In the next few months, I learned a lot watching Christie's demeanor, and I hoped that if my daughter grew up to enter the business world that she would be as capable at such a young age.

The purpose of this first meeting was to explore a foundation for a possible working relationship, and it went great. After the meeting, I was flying so high that I could have flown home without the jet. I got to the office at 3:00 p.m. and walked into the waiting EXCOM meeting to give everyone an update. I went over each idea and got volunteers to investigate a plan and possible procedure for each one. Once again, our executive committee was off and running.

Then I pointed out the other shoe that could drop. "Boys and girls, mommies and daddies," I started, "If we play our cards right and do the job that we are capable of, we will be business partners with Playboy Enterprises. When we do our great job, Playboy is going to love us, and guess what? Playboy is in a very strong cash position once again and is looking for sound investments."

They all began to smile as I continued, "It will make absolute sense for them to invest, say $3 to $5 million in us when they know how professional and productive we are. And of course, that will do two things."

They were nodding in agreement as I went on, "Number one, the stock market will love it and our stock will take a huge jump, and remember that your stock options are at $5. Number two, and more importantly, we will create another potential suitor to compete for us."

"We will be the prettiest girl at the dance, and we'll now have Playboy, Kmart, and a major airline fighting to see who takes us home. How's that for a scenario?" We had one happy executive committee that was totally committed to making our newest project a success.

After the meeting, Ben and I went out for a cold one. I was feeling very proud of this newest business partnership. I bragged to Ben that, although he and our whole team would be getting involved, this one was my baby. This would probably be our last deal this year and I pulled it in.

"The last one this year? Think so?" asked Ben. "By the way, when's the next meeting?"

"They'll be here in two weeks to review plans and possible time tables", I said.

"Two weeks, huh?" replied Ben with this big grin on his face.

"Yeah, two weeks, you'll be in town, won't you?" I asked.

Ben looked like the cat that swallowed the canary. "Oh, I'll be here, but you, Mr. Full-of-Yourself-Bunny-Boy, won't be. You'll be in Puerto Rico."

"See", he continued, "While you were in Chicago working on the old Playboy deal, I was in fact signing our newest last deal of the year. We now have an agreement with Continental and Eastern Airlines to add LeisureLink to their reservation system. You do remember LeisureLink, the leisure travel system, don't you, Mr. Playboy?"

This was an off-the-wall surprise to me. Ben had been working on this deal for six months. We thought that we were making progress with Eastern Airlines, who owned the reservation system. But then Frank Larenzo and Continental bought Eastern and their computerized reservation system, so we had to start over. I thought that there was only an outside chance of a deal, but Ben was the master when it came to negotiating with airlines.

"That's fantastic, Ben!" I jumped up to shake his hand and slap him on the back. "But why will I be in Puerto Rico?"

Ben explained, "They want you to represent them at the annual Caribbean Hotel Association convention. They know that's your group and you know all of the players, so they asked that you to do a presentation on their behalf. So I guess you'll have to force yourself to suck down some rum on our behalf, while Dave and I stay here to review the program progress and possible contract points with Playboy."

The next day I started planning my Puerto Rico presentation, but it felt strange. For the first time, I wasn't excited about heading out to a beautiful resort location. I really wanted to stay home and baby sit my Playboy project, and

I certainly didn't want to miss out on any new ideas. I called Playboy the next day and changed the meeting until the day that I would return from San Juan with an impressive tan (O.K., a nice shade of red).

☆☆☆☆☆☆☆☆☆☆

Now that the meeting date was changed, I could head off to spend quality time in San Juan, Puerto Rico with a positive attitude. It was good catching up with former business associates at the Caribbean Hotel Association, and making new ones. I gave a one hour presentation that was very well received and then I got to settle back to enjoy the festivities. Puerto Rico is known for its fabulous pig roasts and this gala event was no exception. The giant spits turned slowly all day and into the night while the sacrificial pigs were lathered in Puerto Rican spices that flavored the tender meat to perfection. And, ah, the Rum drinks, an unlimited variety, light Rum, dark Rum, and blends of spiced Rum. Part of Puerto Rico's history is that on Christopher Columbus' second voyage to the New World there was a man named Juan Ponce De Leon. Juan feel in love with the area and when Chris returned to Spain, Juan stayed behind. He became Governor of Puerto Rico in 1508. Juan had this obsession with youth and heard stories of the "Fountain of Youth." Its magical liquid would keep one young forever. Juan searched for years and supposedly found nothing. Much later, the people of Puerto Rico built a noble statue of Governor Ponce De Leon with his outstretched arm, pointing toward the elusive fountain. The remarkable thing is that the statue points directly to the Puerto Rican Fountain of Youth, only a quarter of a mile away, yes, Juan's statue is pointing directly to the Bacardi Rum distillery.

We enjoyed vast quantities of Juan's tonic. It is amazing how this magic elixir can make you feel so young and invincible all night long, and yet so very old and feeble the very next morning.

☆☆☆☆☆☆☆☆☆☆

Two days after my return, we hosted Christie Hefner and her new Playboy project team. Christie had, naturally, been all over the world and owned a property in Aspen, so we decided to forego trying to impress her with our little corner of Colorado.

Rather, we spent our time trying to impress her with our employees and the fact that our team was extremely capable of creating highly successful programs for Playboy.

It was a very comfortable and productive meeting, and they left with the knowledge that we knew our stuff and could be strong business partners.

Through our discussions, we found that one of the ways that Playboy Enterprises had made tons of money was through their Playboy Club Casinos. Though few in numbers, they were extremely profitable in their time. Playboy still had an interest in gaming if the right venue could be found.

The next day at our EXCOM update meeting, Ben and I laid out the Playboy Gaming idea before the committee. Limited stakes gaming had not yet begun, so there was only Las Vegas and Atlantic City, with their giant casinos. How could we make something work?

The EXCOM kept saying, "We don't know anything about gambling." They were right. We didn't know gambling, we knew travel, resorts and cruises.

After a fruitless hour of throwing ideas on the wall and nothing sticking, Bill Lever, now president of our new cruise franchise division, got this huge smile on his face, and screamed, "Hold it everyone, I think we can make this thing float!"

"Ah float, I love it when you use that fancy cruise talk", Dave joked.

"Well, float this", Bill grinned, "Playboy knows gaming and we know cruising. Vegas and Atlantic City are not viable right now, so what if we created a casino cruise ship?"

Bill explained to us that in Europe they have these huge ferry boats that do eight hour trips between ports. The ships have five levels of parking and the main deck is a floating shopping mall with movie theatres and even sleeping cabins that can be rented. So, what if we reconfigured one of these to make a floating Playboy Club Casino?

Bill's wise words primed the pump, and once again the ideas started flowing, and soon kicked into turbo drive.

It could be legal anywhere. All we'd have to do is sail out past the twelve mile limit and the covers would come off the gaming tables.

Where would we sail from?

Would it be just an eight hour gambling cruise to nowhere, or should we design a complete cruise ship that would do complete three to seven day cruises.

We could design first class cabins in a Playboy Club motif.

Here's a great one, the anchors could be giant Rabbit Heads.

Once again, like our other idea sessions, we spent hours throwing out ideas and writing everything down.

Out of the meeting came a new proposal to present to Playboy Enterprises: The Playboy Casino Cruise Club. The first step to the plan was a trip to Helsinki, Finland, the home of one of the world's largest ship builders, Wort Sila. Ben and Bill met with Wort Sila to see how a giant ferry boat could be retrofitted into a floating casino, and how much it would cost. If this could work, it would be a huge project, even for the likes of Playboy. They returned in a week with several designs, working plans, proposals and cost estimates. The next two weeks were spent developing sales plans and projections as the next step in the development of a comprehensive business plan to present to

Playboy. It would be a multimillion dollar project that would reap huge rewards for all. Success is an extremely powerful drug and I had become a happy and willing addict. I was on a non-stop high and dreaming of getting higher.

12

The Gathering

I t was May, 1987, springtime in the Rockies, and we were enjoying the great outdoors as a company. We joined a coed softball league and put together our team. This was a fun leisure league with the teams made up half guys and half gals, and you batted boy, girl, boy, girl. The purpose of this league was to just have fun. The league didn't know about us. Oh, we always knew how to have fun, but no matter what the game, we came to win. The women on our team were not only talented business professionals; they were better athletes than some of the guys. Whether mountain biking, whitewater kayaking, or downhill skiing, these ladies were at the top of their form. By our third game, we were being accused of bringing in "ringers". We won every game and the tourney. After being awarded our trophy, we were told that next year we would have to play in the competitive league. Ah, the penalty of success.

With June came our first anniversary of going public and we were going to celebrate. We planned a huge all day family picnic. We invited all family members and friends, our travel agencies, investors, and business partners. Everyone there had a part in our success and this was the well deserved thank you event.

We wanted to have an old fashioned family picnic, and set up committees to plan the details. In addition to the pig roast, we had tons of other food that everyone would like. Along with sack races and three legged races, we had softball, volleyball, badminton, frisbee, horseshoes, water balloons, and just about anything else people could hit, throw or kick. We would make sure that there was fun for everyone, especially the kids. We thought of any little silly thing that would make the kids have fun and remember the day. Every kid won something for any event, even the watermelon seed spitting contest. I finished third, behind two six year olds, but I still contend that they cheated.

I absolutely love kids. I blocked out the grownup activities and just sat back and watched all of these kids playing and laughing. I am constantly delighted by kids' boundless excitement and enthusiasm. Kids have this uninhibited ability to enjoy life, and what they're doing in it, openly and without reservations. One of the greatest sounds in life is a kid's laughter. As I watched them, I realized how lucky I was to be a part of this company of fantastic people. The parents of these kids had the same contagious enthusiasm in building our company that their kids had in play. It was an unbridled exuberance of enjoying what they were doing and sharing it with each other.

I've found that in life, we sometimes act as

though comfort and the acquiring of "stuff" are the chief requirements of life, and the reason we get out of bed in the morning. But what we really quite simply need is something to be enthusiastic about. Hanging in my office was a plaque with a quote of James Michener that read,

"The master in the art of living makes no distinction between his work and his play, his labor and his leisure, his mind and his body, his information and recreation, his life and religion. He rarely knows which is which. He simply pursues his vision of excellence at whatever he does, leaving others to decide whether he is working or playing. To him, he is always doing both."

That quote pretty well summed up everyone in our company, and I was bursting with pride to think that I was part of this.

Everyone gathered around to eat and I made a toast, welcoming everyone and thanking them for their dedication and hard work in making the company a success. Ben followed my toast with a nice one of his own, then finished by saying, "And now for desert first, I'd like you all to know that Kmart is very very very satisfied with our performance and they just informed me that they are going to invest $3 million in us!"

As everyone cheered and raised their cups, I thought what an incredible anniversary gift to finish an incredible year.

As the picnic wore gently into the night, I couldn't wipe the smile off of my face or from my heart. In one year we had created something that had never been done in the travel industry, and along with it we had helped build a quality life for our employees and their families in the wonderland of Colorado.

Ben and I had started with little more than an idea and enthusiasm. We spent just about every dollar we had getting this thing going. We went from introducing an automated travel system, to taking the company public, to acquiring the largest travel agency franchise company in the nation and increasing revenues to $500 million, to creating a new means of distribution through Kmart, to creating a whole new franchise company for cruise only stores, to the first travel magazine, to a business partnership with Playboy Enterprises. Whew, if you're worn out just reading that sentence, think what it did to us achieving it all in one year! Success beyond our wildest dreams was ours, and we had only just begun. Could the next year even come close to what we accomplished in this first year? Would we double our size? What new frontiers in travel could we conquer? Would we grow so strong that someone would try to buy us ahead of our planned schedule? Whatever our future would hold, I knew it was going be unbelievable.

13

Cash Begins With K

After Ben's announcement that Kmart was willing to make a $3 million investment in us, we started to prepare for the next steps. The procedure would be that Kmart would send their investment team to complete their due diligence of us before they would invest the money. If everything went to plan, we would sign off on the investment and get the money in mid July. In late June, they spent a week with us, going over our books and meeting our people. They left satisfied that we were a solid investment. A week later, Ben, Dave and Ed got together with Kmart's attorneys in Troy, Michigan to draw up the documents.

While they were gone, I cranked up my publicity mill. I made phone calls to people that I knew well in the stock industry and created excitement by sharing what I could, within SEC guidelines. By July 1st, our stock was at $13 and rising.

I also made a call to a contact that I had at INC. Magazine. As part of an ongoing PR campaign, I had been sending this columnist all of the press clippings about our successes, and kept lobbying for a feature article about us in INC. I called him regularly to say hello, and blatantly ask when we were going to be on the cover. He found the Kmart news to be exciting, and coupled with our other successes, he was now finally ready to discuss a feature article. We left the conversation with a tentative meeting in the first week of August to begin the article.

When the guys got back from Kmart's headquarters, they had more good news. From their discussions with the Kmart brass, they each felt that Kmart was seriously thinking about buying us in the future.

The closing date to finalize everything and get the money was set for July 15. This $3 million investment was a baby step for Kmart, and nothing more than a tiny drop from their very big bucket. They could sneeze $3 million and not miss it, but it was huge for us. We needed the additional working capital to keep our new programs afloat until they could stand on their own.

We started to calculate an estimate of what Global Group could be worth in one year. Ben's CPA brain, Dave's corporate and SEC legal brain, and Ed's stock market analyst's brain were whirling, and giving me a headache. This was exciting for me to watch, because my little marketing right brain was incapable of such calculations. They spent over two hours playing "what if" with all the variables. The best conservative "guesstimate" was that if each of our new divisions and programs succeeded as planned, our new little company would be conservatively valued at between $180 to $200 million by the end of 1988. We shook our heads in amusement as we shared the vision of several suitors outbidding each other for us. This investment in us by Kmart was the first step down the alter with someone, and whoever it was going to be, we were looking forward to saying "I Do".

On July 14, our stock had risen to $18, and we were on a jet to Detroit. We got in Tuesday evening so we'd be fresh for our morning drive to Kmart's corporate headquarters in Troy.

✩✩✩✩✩✩✩✩✩✩

The next morning we met at 10:00 to give them an update on the travel program, and then review the investment documents. Everything was in order, but instead of signing then and there, the Kmart folks first wanted to take us to lunch with Kmart's Senior VP, Jim Anthony.

We sat through lunch politely chatting, all the time thinking to ourselves "Give us the check". Finally lunch was over and we headed back to the conference room to sign off on everything and head home with $3 million.

Well, that was the plan.

14

Was That With A B?

When we retuned to the conference room, Mr. Anthony was called out by one of the attorneys. Since he was the one who would be signing, we sat there like impatient kids at Christmas, waiting for mom and dad to come downstairs so we could open our presents.

Twenty minutes later, he came back in the room and announced, "Gentlemen, we have a problem."

"Problem?" asked Dave, "The documents looked fine to us."

"Yes, the documents are all in order and we want to do this deal with you, but..."

I swear that time froze as the word "but" fell from his lips. In that split second between "but" and whatever his next word would be, my mind was screaming, "BUT? BUT? There's no stinkin' BUT here. This is a done deal, give us our damn check!"

I snapped back to reality and the rest of his sentence...

"But," he continued, "We have all just been served with a lawsuit."

"A lawsuit? What do you mean a lawsuit? Who would sue us? What kind of a lawsuit?", Dave fired the legal questions at the room.

"Gentlemen, Global Group and its officers, and Kmart and its officers have just been sued for $1.4 Billion."

We sat in stunned, paralyzing silence. After an eternity, I began babbling, "Whoa there a minute, did you just say BILLION, like with a B? I could have sworn that you said Billion, but you meant million, right? You didn't say Billion. I could've sworn I heard Billion but it had to be million."

"No, I said Billion because I meant to say Billion," snapped Anthony. He then added, "John will explain it to you; I've got another meeting to run to." And with that, he walked out. Oh, that's fun, toss the kids a nuclear bomb and then leave.

John was one of Kmart's head attorneys and he stood before us with the newly received lawsuit in hand. He handed a copy to Dave, who immediately dove into a speed reading frenzy. John explained that the lawsuit was filed against us by two of our travel agency franchisees. Among the charges was licensing infringement, antitrust violation and racketeering.

Once again, we were stunned. There was this tremendous flash of anxiety that felt like a blast in the face with a blow torch. I didn't know if I was going to vomit or just pass out.

John tried to continue, but Ben interrupted, "Antitrust violation? Racketeering? It sounds like something from an Elliot Ness versus Al Capone movie. What in hell are these people talking about? And why $1.4 Billion?"

We all chimed in at once, jabbering in high pitched voices of confused panic.

John stood silent, patiently waiting for everyone to calm back down, then continued, "If we can all try to stay calm, we can get through this. I've only had this thing for an hour, so we'll all go through it together. Let me finish explaining what I know and what our strategy will be."

We all took deep breaths and prepared to listen. John explained that the lawsuit appeared to contend that if Global and Kmart enter into an agreement to sell travel, we would be in direct competition with our franchised travel agencies in their locations, thus infringing on their licensing rights.

Dave pointed out that this was not the case because we had included a provision that would actually pay our agencies a commission on any sales made. The true bottom line would be that the agencies would be making additional money for doing nothing.

"I agree with your premise, Dave," answered John. "At first glance the lawsuit appears to be without merit. But as an attorney yourself, you know that you don't have to be right to file a lawsuit."

Ben impatiently brought up the B word again, "John, why $1.4 Billion?"

John gave a slight smile and replied, "My guess is that they've got an attorney that wants to get our attention, and it worked. Using $1.4 billion, instead of an even $1.5 gives the impression that they actually performed some sort of calculations."

He continued, "Gentlemen, it really boils down to a few simple things. Because of our size, we get sued, sometimes on a daily basis. Someone buys a lawn mower, cuts his toe off and sues us. Someone else buys a kiddie pool and leaves their kid alone in it and sues us when the kid drowns. The list goes on and on and on. There have been a few times when a lawsuit had merit, most times not. This is America, land of the easy lawsuit, and attorneys looking for a quick cash settlement, whether they have a case or not."

"In this case, these people chose a huge amount because we're Kmart. We're the second largest retailer in the world. We have over 2,100 stores and $22 Billion in sales, and they think we're an easy bank to rob. Well, they are very, very wrong."

Hmm, "they are very very wrong." I liked the sound of that. "So, John," I interrupted, "You're saying that there's going to be a battle here."

"Oh yeah," John responded with an intensely, determined look, "There's going to be more than a battle. It will be a war. Since we're both named in the lawsuit, this will be a joint response, and this is how it will work."

"First, we do not settle bullshit lawsuits like this one. We have a full staff of attorneys who do nothing but litigation."

"Second, we will crush these little cockroaches and make an example out of them. I anticipate filing several counter suits against them that could tie up their time and money for years. I can confidently say that we will not only put a stop to what appears to be their little extortion game, but we will probably bankrupt them in the process."

We all sat with big smiles on our faces while sighs of relief began to replace the anxiety and fear that was making our hearts race. I suddenly felt like that little kid back in Indiana. Just when I thought that I was going to get beat up by a bully, my big brother came out of nowhere and pounded him into the ground.

There was no question that John and his staff knew this game well, and played only to win. Ben and I listened intently for the next hour while Dave and John discussed legal issues and procedures. Wrapping up his assessment, John asked, "Dave, as Global's corporate counsel, you and I will be spending quite a bit of time on this. Any other questions for now?"

"Not about the lawsuit," said Dave. "You've got our commitment to help in any way to get this thing over. That being said, can we get back to signing off on our agreement so we can still make our plane back to Denver?"

John looked a bit surprised. "The agreement? Gentlemen, I'm sure that you understand that we want to finalize our agreement and make the $3 million investment in Global. But surely you also understand that under the circumstances, we cannot go forward at this point. We will first have to complete a full review of this lawsuit and possible implications."

Back in panic mode, I pleaded, "But we have a completed agreement."

John didn't blink, "I'm sorry gentlemen, but because of this new situation, as of now we have only a pending agreement that will simply be put on hold. My hope is that we can get a handle on the suit in the next sixty days and perhaps move forward. But for know, all I can tell you is that I wish that I could hand you the check for $3 million, but I can't...and I won't."

I felt like that Indiana kid again, only this time instead of the bully, my big brother decided to beat me up.

We boarded our return flight with our papers in hand, only instead of a signed agreement and a check for $3 million; we were carrying documents for a lawsuit for $1.4 Billion. Instead of heading home with much needed working capital to continue our growth, we were heading into murky uncharted waters with an unknown course. We sat in pained silence, each of us playing out possible scenarios in our minds, hoping to stumble upon some brilliant resolution to our predicament.

Finally, Ben said, "Well, guys, I think that the first thing we should do is meet with Jack," and with that he caught the flight attendant's attention. We met with Jack Daniels all the way back to Denver. He didn't help a bit.

15

Fasten Your Seat Belts

The next morning, we got to the office at 6:30 a.m. to get busy on our stories; the explanations to our employees, franchisees, investors, and the press.

Our employees started our day with mixed emotions. On the outside of our building was a huge handmade banner that shouted "Welcome Home! Thanks For Everything!" Ben's assistant, Anne came in at 7:00 and informed us that a celebration party was planned for the afternoon to "Hail Our Conquering Heros". I thought that by the end of the day it might be, "To Hell with the blundering morons".

Boy, it was going to be a long day.

We stayed in the conference room, with the door closed, reviewing strategies. The first thing was to call for an executive committee meeting at 8:30 and a company wide meeting for 9:00. Ben and I started reviewing our remarks, which we unfortunately had to share with our wives the night before. This would be the first time that we had to stand in front of our wonderful team with anything less that great news, and we hoped that it would be the last.

Our employees burst into the meetings, excited and joking about what they thought was the good news that they were going to hear. It was tough watching the smiling faces of our people turn to confused looks of worry and dismay as we began explaining our predicament. We attempted to be as positive as possible, but we also were upfront with everyone that this could create a severe cash crunch within the next sixty days if it were not resolved. We reminded everyone that, while this situation was working itself out, it was still business as usual in all other areas. One of the guys piped up, "So, if it's business as usual, the party's still on for today?"

"You know what? I think that's a great idea," Ben answered. "By the end of today we can all use a party, as long as it not a lynching party."

Before the meeting ended, we also explained the implications of what a $1.4 Billion lawsuit could do to our company stock. That's why Dave was not in the meetings. He was busy writing an announcement to the press that would be released jointly by Global and Kmart before noon to satisfy SEC regulations. One of the strictest SEC regulations on a publicly held company is a thing called "disclosure". Basically, what this means is that a company must disclose any derogatory information that may have a negative impact on the company's performance, which in turn could have a negative impact on the price of the stock. This disclosure must be made "at once", which means that you can't sit around hoping that things will get better. No sir, you've got to climb to the top of the mountain and shout at the top of your lungs, "Hey World! Guess what? We just got sued for $1.4 BILLION!"

The joint release went out over the wire services at 10:00 a.m. This was just what the stock market wanted to hear about our new little company. By the end of business the next day on Friday, our stock dropped from its high of $18.00 to $12.00. Needless to say, we were not looking forward to what the next week might bring.

As Bette Davis said in the movie, *All about Eve*, "You better fasten your seat belts, it's going to be a bumpy ride."

16

Who Wants This Call?

We spent Saturday and most of Sunday at the office, home of our newest corporate division: the Crisis Command Center. After reviewing the lawsuit again and again, we started planning for the phone calls that we knew would start at 6:00 a.m. on Monday. We knew that we would be deluged from investors, stock companies, and our travel agency franchisees. We also had to be prepared for the onslaught of media; local news media, regional and national business press, and the travel trade press.

Our plan was to start out on Monday by proactively calling the east coast stock firms in an attempt to diffuse fears. Next, around 7:30, we would start handling incoming calls. Dave would handle stock and investor calls, Ben would take the travel agency and airline calls, and I would handle the press and local media, Playboy, our publishing company and other miscellaneous calls.

We called Melanie, our executive office manager at home and asked her to please come in by 7:00 a.m. Mel was a tiger under pressure. We would need her expertise handling what we knew would be a heavy incoming call volume.

Mel had a college degree, was incredibly organized, could run the computers at burn-up speed, and loved to handle our executive duties. Over the phone she spoke with a smooth pleasing voice that could calm the beasts that would be calling. Outside of work, she dated a Harley biker, threw down beers and shots of tequila that would put us all under the table, and swore like a sailor.

Ben, Dave and I got to the office at 6:00 Monday morning. As we walked in, the lights were on, the Grateful Dead was playing loudly and we could smell fresh coffee. Out of the kitchen came Mel, with a pot of coffee in one hand and our three mugs in the other. As we looked at each other and laughed, Mel poured our coffee and greeted us with, "Good morning, Boys, are we ready to kick some ass today?"

"Mel", said Ben, "we asked if you could come in at 7:00, not 6:00."

"Yeah, righteo, big boss man," she retorted in typical Mel fashion. "You think I was going to miss the opening act of this action thriller?" In a corporate crisis, and probably a bar fight, we were glad to have Mel on our side.

Before we could settle in to start calling out, the lines started lighting up. Mel killed the music and shouted, "Gentlemen, it's show time, and I believe I have some incoming shit aiming to hit your fans!" We gave Mel a thirty second briefing on how best to direct the calls to us, and ran for our offices, leaving our doors open in case we had to shout to each other. Inside of ten minutes, our proactive call plans were tossed aside as we moved to the reactive mode of answering calls that were on hold. They were coming in fast and furious, and the operative word for many was furious.

"What in hell is going on? What have you dolts done to the stock?" Ah yes, we loved intelligent questions from reasonable people, and I wanted to offer solid answers like, "Well, you see, we were afraid of making any real money, so we thought we would do a bunch of illegal things so we could get sued for a whole lot of money so your stock would be worthless. Then we would all laugh as you went broke and we went out of business. This was our intent from the beginning and by golly, we're right on track. So thanks for calling and have a nice day."

As our lines stayed full, the three of us would occasionally get off the phone at the same time and scream to Mel, "Who's on which line?"

To break the tension and cool us down, she switched into her Mel mode and started throwing us calls by announcing in her sweetest smoothest sexiest voice, "Oh, Davey, I have Mr. Jones, the world's most powerful stock broker and legend in his own mind on line one. And please be reminded that we have only one priority in life, and that would be him."

"Benny dearest, I have the most utterly annoyed and distressed Mr. Smith of D. P. Edwards, better known to us as the giant puss seeping pimple on the butt of the world, on line three. He would like to remind us all that he has been on hold three times and is much much too important for this."

"And Stevie, on line four I have holding for you, that ridiculous pant load for brains, lacking in all writing skills or sense of financial reason, from the Denver Business News, weighing in with an I. Q. of 37, Mr. Jim Atkins."

Ah, good ol' Mel, always to the point.

We worked the phones nonstop until noon. We choked down some sandwiches in the conference room while deciding how to get back on track. We decided that we each had three calls that we had to make before taking any other urgent ones, at the same time realizing that we were in a triage mode for urgent incoming calls. Occasionally, Mel would announce a call from a real pain with, "And now boys, who wants *this* call?" We would run into the hallway and flip a coin for odd man out. By 9:00 p.m. Monday evening, we finally got off the phones and into a cold drink. The most important mission of the day had been completed; to protect the price of our stock. I learned that in the stock broker investment industry there is no reality, there is only their *perception* of reality. If their perception is negative, then our stock dives, no matter what. So, we explained over and over to stock firms that we felt that the $1.4 billion lawsuit was frivolous and would be thrown out, and that our attorneys would know the next step in about three weeks, and to please just hang in there for awhile. Defining "awhile" was not the easiest thing to do. For a stock broker, awhile could mean that he would lose his position if he didn't dump our stock before someone else did. We were trying our best to assure them that the best bet was to hang in with us, and we'd get through this, but deep down we knew that if we were in their shoes, we'd be dumping our stock. If they sold it now and got out on the down side, they could always jump back in after we settled the lawsuit and the stock started back up again. This was a logical position…for them, not us. We knew that a few big sell orders would start a snowball rolling downhill that we probably would not be able to stop. We had weathered the first storm, but knew there were going to be many more.

For the next three weeks, we handled calls in a nonstop, but more organized and civilized fashion. We were able to maintain our stock price at about $11.00, so our "wait for awhile and hang in there" strategy had worked so far.

We also gave our employees daily updates to keep everyone up to speed on any new events. Our time was being taken away from the day to day running of the company, so our great EXCOM and all employees picked up the slack without being asked. But that was the kind of people they were, selfless and dedicated.

17

Waiter, This Is Not What I Ordered

It was now mid August, a month from the filing of the lawsuit. We were trying to get back to normal, while the attorneys were still sorting out legal strategy. We had to stay on track and had many projects proceeding. We did our best to keep reassuring the investment community to please be patient, but our stock kept slipping. By August 15, it had dropped to $8 and showed no reason that it would stay there.

We were in the final planning stage for our upcoming annual travel agency owners' convention in mid September. It was going to be held on a seven day cruise onboard the newest and biggest ship of Carnival Cruise Lines. We expected a group of 500 people, and had developed many training seminars for the franchisees and their key agents that would be held at sea, between fun port excursions and play time in Cozumel, Grand Cayman, and Ocho Rios, Jamaica.

We knew that some of the attendees would be coming with very bad attitudes so we wanted all of the positive things possible to present to our franchisees to overcome the negative feelings of the lawsuit.

We also knew that the number one topic to

address would be the lawsuit and how it would affect our franchisees. We would be proceeding with the convention without a conclusion to the lawsuit and we had to address it right up front, in a very matter of fact way, and hopefully take it off of the table for the rest of the week. As we got closer to the sailing date, we put all of our agency support staff through role playing so they would be aware of how to handle a week's worth of questions. The good news about a seven day cruise was that our staff could spend a lot of quality one on one time with our travel agents to strengthen our positive relationship with them. The bad news was that if we have some people on the war path, you can't get away from them. We instructed our staff that if they were blindsided by an angry or disruptive person, to turn them over to us at once so we could hopefully diffuse the situation early and keep things on a positive course.

We were also wrapping up the premier issue of LeisureLink, the World's Leisure Travel Magazine. It was taking great shape and after final editing, it was going to press in the first week of September. We had Rio on the cover and enticing photographs and articles about Rio's Carnival, Colorado skiing, the Caribbean, Hawaii, cruising the Panama Canal, and travel tips galore. I've got to say that it was a kick to see my name in print as the "Publisher", as well as my new column on "Travel Trends". We would have samples in time to make a splashy presentation at the cruise convention.

LeisureLink, the magazine would become a dynamic sales tool for the agencies as well as a high quality image builder. Every destination written about was a vacation that could be booked through our agencies, which should make everyone happy. We developed a press kit to build local PR, and planned a session on how best to use the magazines to promote the individual agencies businesses in their communities.

We were also planning the introduction of our new cruise only retail stores. We had opened the test store in Kansas City with one of our largest franchisees, and it was getting rave reviews. Located in a large shopping mall, it was designed to look like the inside of a ship. We even had a gangplank that you crossed to enter the store. We not only had cruise experts available to discuss cruising, but each month we would have a different cruise line set up a display and promote specials. Prospective cruisers could check out free videos about cruise destinations. The new concept quite simply worked.

We were originally going to introduce the concept as a whole new and separate franchise company, offering this new idea to our agency franchisees first. But after the lawsuit, we were afraid that it might create a bad feeling among the current franchisees. Some of them might accuse us of attempting to compete directly with them again. So we changed our direction for the time being, and decided to introduce the store as the International Travel Partners Cruise Aweigh stores. We were going to present two concepts: the completely designed retail store as originally planned, and now were going to add a Cruise Aweigh department within our existing travel agency locations. Either way, we would help our agencies sell more high margin cruises and make more money.

Another prototype that we were introducing was our mini-agency located inside a major grocery chain. We had completed a successful test with another of our large franchisees and the results were very positive. This new area of distribution and sale of travel products was unique to the industry and had great growth potential. It would also demonstrate the commitment to our franchisee to constantly strive to develop new methods to increase their sales and bottom line profits. We felt that we had the new programs and training seminars that were going to create the most productive and successful owners' convention in the twenty years that ITP had been in business.

☆☆☆☆☆☆☆☆☆☆

As we were concentrating on making the convention a huge success, we were faced with two setbacks in two days.

First, Kmart notified us that they were still very interested in doing business with us and investing in us, but they didn't want to generate any bad publicity in the interim by continuing

the program while the legal proceedings
continued. Ouch! This was not what we wanted
to hear. The reality was that this deal was so
minor to Kmart that it was not worth them
messing with for now. I could understand their
thinking, but couldn't agree with it. For
whatever time the "interim" was, we were left
with huge overhead for the reservation center
and personnel...and we were left with no cash.

Second, Playboy called to say basically the
same thing. They liked our company, and our
creative plans. They wanted to proceed, they
really did, but would not until any possible
legalities were totally cleared up. They were
back in the black and were not going to
jeopardize anything by possibly getting
connected to our lawsuit. They reassured us that
they were not going to look elsewhere, they were
just going to shelve the plans for now.

Ah, the best laid plans. Well, excuse me waiter,
this is not what I ordered.

While putting on our most positive face for
our franchisees, our airline partners, and the
investment community, we knew that we were
approaching a world of financial hurt. We would
have to raise working capital to keep things
going and growing. Since we had absolutely no
idea how long the lawsuit might drag on, we
reasoned that we would need to raise $1 to $3
million in the next thirty to forty five days.

So, here we were again, trying to run a
growing company while trying to raise funds;
once again splitting our time in different

directions.

There was also one huge problem. It's not exactly the easiest thing in the world to try to raise money when you're in the middle of a $1.4 Billion lawsuit. Luckily for us, Ed called to say hi from Seattle. In talking to him, Ben found that he was not happy in Seattle and wanted to get back to his family in Colorado. This was great timing, because we needed his expertise at raising money. We set up an office and the next week he was back with us and got busy searching for interim financing.

Ben was spending most of his time with Ed and Dave on this crisis, so I tried to concentrate my full time on "business as usual". Ed and Dave started working their networks across the nation in the hope of finding an entity that would look at our situation and see a financing opportunity. They felt if they could just find two or three companies that wanted to get into the travel industry that we could get our necessary funding. Ed and Dave stayed on the phones and made meeting appointments tirelessly.

It was not an easy sell. Current investors would not touch us. Before someone new would invest, they would have to complete a very thorough due diligence which would include meeting with our Global –Kmart combined legal staff. No one would possibly invest with the chance of their investment just going into a lawsuit settlement pot. They would have to feel confident that the lawsuit would be dismissed down the road, which would make their investment a wise one indeed. But quite honestly, we knew it was a crap shoot.

By the first week of September, we though that we had hit a home run. Ed found a company that wanted to enter the travel industry. They understood the upside and after doing their due diligence, decided that the upside outweighed the possible downside. They would submit their proposal to invest $1.5 million to their board on September 7. When approved, we could close on the deal on September 28.

Ben, Dave and Ed had pulled out the impossible and we would soon be at full throttle again...or maybe not.

Late in the afternoon, September 7, we received the call. The company's board of directors soundly rejected the proposal as "bad business and unthinkable". This was a smack in the face, even though deep down, we each silently agreed with them. It's hard to argue with logic and this reaction was unfortunately a very logical one. It was also one that we would get over and over again.

18

Man Overboard

D espite the setback, we had to head to Miami the next week to board our cruise ship to the Caribbean for our seven day floating convention. Dave and Ed stayed behind to keep working on the money, while Ben and I put on our happy faces and became the perfect corporate hosts for this very important meeting with almost 500 travel agency owners and their key personnel. A meeting this big was quite an organizational undertaking, but our agency support staff and our cruise experts had done an incredible job of planning every small detail. On a seven day cruise, you alternate a day at sea with a day at a different port, so we would hold morning sessions, ever other day while at sea and then play and enjoy the land destinations.

We set sail on Saturday afternoon with a big gala welcoming party that went into the evening. We held off any individual questions about the lawsuit, explaining that this would be the first and foremost topic at our general session Monday morning.

The next morning, I started the session with some trivial light hearted comments about the wonderful time we were all going to have over the next week and how many new tools for success everyone was going to go home with. The crowd sat politely, waiting for substance, so I introduced Ben. This time there was no stage fright because Ben was on a mission to get the facts out on the table and get it behind us. He reviewed the lawsuit. Yes, it had been filed by two of our travel agency franchisees, and no, we do not believe that it has any merit whatsoever, and here's why. With overhead support materials, he explained in precise detail what the agreement was with Kmart and how it was going to benefit every agency owner, not hurt them.

He then presented two closers, a copy showing that both agencies were behind in their fees to us in the amount of about $100,000, and finally a copy of a letter from their attorneys to ours that they would settle for a mere $10 million. Ben stared straight at the crowd with a defiant look and stated firmly, "Let me make this as absolutely crystal clear as possible to each and every one of you. Kmart and Global Group will not play what is quite simply a game of extortion." The crowd applauded in support and Ben finished them off. "You know, Steve and I went through an earthquake with most of you two years ago, and we'll all get through this. We are working to put this behind us and we are asking for your support. I've told you everything there is to tell and I am now done discussing it. If some of you came on board to create a conflict during this week, I suggest that you get off at the first port, because this week is going to be about making your agencies more successful and ways to make you more money."

The crowd appreciated Ben's straight forward approach and many actually gave him a standing ovation. The speech set the tone for a positive and constructive week to come. Ben turned the meeting over to our agency support team and our convention was off and running, with a morning and early afternoon full of sessions on how to be more successful.

The day ran smoothly, with training breakout sessions that were fully attended and well received. We ended our sessions by 1:00 p.m. so everyone could enjoy the cruise.

The next day we landed in Cozumel, which is well known as a diving destination. It is home to the world famous Palancar Reef, which treats divers to the sight of thousands of brilliantly colored fish. Non-divers spent a fun day beach combing, sight seeing and shopping. Our time was spent schmoozing our franchisees. We had our key personnel split up and spend leisure time with various groups of our agency owners. After a fun and productive day, we got back to the ship around midnight. As we slept, the ship set sail onward toward Grand Cayman Island.

When Ben and I got back to our cabin, there was a message waiting from Dave. He and Ed had two very positive meetings that might actually turn into money, and wanted to discuss it ASAP. It was hard to sleep while wondering about the phone call that we would make the next morning. We called the ship's concierge to arrange a ship to shore call for 9:00 a.m., which would allow us to kick off the morning session and then slip out for the call.

Ed had made previous contact with a company in Los Angeles and had sent them the "due dilly" info. That was followed with a conference call with their legal people and Ed and Dave. They wanted to get into the travel industry and understood the lawsuit implications. A meeting was needed ASAP because their CEO was leaving the country at the end of the week, and would be gone for a few weeks. It was Tuesday and we were at sea, somewhere between Cozumel and Grand Cayman, and could do nothing for now. Ben told Dave, "We'll dock Wednesday morning in Grand Cayman. Have Anne work out the details to get me a flight to L. A. and set the meeting, I'll be there."

I had two seminars to do on Friday so I would have to stay on board and keep up the good front while Ben jumped ship and headed for possible money. I rode with him to the airport and we joked that hopefully his meeting would succeed. If not he would call me and for a grand finale of the cruise, I could walk the plank.

I dropped Ben at the airport and headed back to meet and treat a group of franchisees to a perfect day of snorkeling in the sparkling turquoise waters of Grand Cayman. I actually relaxed a bit as we spent peaceful hours swimming with the multicolored tropical fish and a few curious stingrays. We then mellowed out into the evening, lounging on the powder-soft sand of the beautiful Seven Mile Beach that is enhanced with the shade of palm trees and hammocks. As I was sipping anything with tequila in it and making sure that everyone was having a good time, my thoughts kept slipping to Ben, who was hopefully on his way to save me from walking the plank. Because of our sailing schedule and the poor quality of the ship-to-shore phone system, I would probably not hear anything until I got home, so all I could do was hope.

Our last stop was a day in Ocho Rios, Jamaica, where many of us climbed up the famous Dunn's River Falls. This is a 600 foot high natural staircase of cascading water with deep cool whirlpools to relax and play in as through the falling water to the top. As I was climbing up, I realized that this was one more reason that we had to get our survival money; I quite simply loved the travel industry and the people in it.

The rest of the cruise went well, though people occasionally wondered where Ben was. We just explained that he fell overboard. Our presentation of our new magazine *LeisureLink* and the CRUISE AWEIGH stores were both enthusiastically received. The travel agency owners understood the marketing impact that we were working so hard to create and fully understood that our new plans would bring them increased business and bottom line profits. The final night onboard we had one last party with everyone that ran until 1:00 a.m. I then quietly gathered up all of our staff and suggested that we all slip away to the darkness and seclusion of the very top deck. This particular deck is hidden away because during the day it is a clothes free sun deck secluded from curious eyes. At night it offers the most spectacular views of a starlit night. I bribed a bar manager to transfer an entire stock of adult beverages to the deck without being seen. Our staff told no one and slipped away in secret to our own private party where we would watch the sun rise over the ocean. I wanted this time with each of them because we had all been so busy and now it was their time. I also wanted the time because deep down, I had a feeling that this opportunity may not happen again. Everyone just kicked backed and relaxed, not having to worry about entertaining others. I silently watched them just being themselves, a terrific group of caring, talented people, who through this week had become even more bonded to each other. I smiled as I realized that this is as good as it gets.

We had accomplished all of our goals for the convention. As we docked back at our Miami port the mood of our franchisees was one of positive cohesiveness and strong support of our people and our programs. After hand shakings, hugs, goodbyes and thank yous, I was one of the last ones off of the ship and I ran for a phone to call Ben.

As soon as Ben answered, I said, "You better have some good news, because I'm off the ship and away from the plank."

"You can stay dry for awhile", Ben laughed, and then explained that the meeting actually went quite well. So well, in fact that Dave and Ed were working on preliminary documents that would be reviewed upon the return of the company's CEO when he returned to his office on October 5th. We would be looking at somewhere between $1 to $1.5 million.

"I think we've got a real good chance on this one", said Ben. "Have a good flight back, get some rest and we'll talk tomorrow." I let out a huge sigh and flagged down a cab for the airport. Between relief from Ben's call and a bit of a hangover from watching the sunrise on the top deck, (yeah, it was the rising sun, not the booze) I finally relaxed and slept all the flight back to Denver.

19

The Bastards
Won't Defeat Us

Monday, I got the rest of the story from Ben and it sounded very encouraging. The company was a privately held real estate firm that had been diversifying by investing in public companies. They had a very successful year and Ben sold them on the upside of the travel industry.

For many companies, the travel Industry had a certain sex appeal because in addition to it being a growing industry, they would get to travel to exotic places for business. They were impressed that Ben left the top cruise ship in the world just to meet with them. Details of the investment were proceeding nicely and it looked very positive.

So, meanwhile, back to business. The rest of the week was spent recapping the successful convention, and doing all of the necessary follow up with the attendees. We had developed a press kit and presented it to each agency owner and reviewed how they should generate local news releases about the convention, while I contacted the trade press for national news. This part of our business was sound and was moving forward.

While I was on the cruise there was more good

news. Ed had also met with a capital firm in Seattle and felt that they were interested as well. They were a public company with a tightly controlled board of directors that basically did what they were told. Ben, Dave and Ed were going to see them the following week and push for a minimum of $1 million.

We also had one more ace up our sleeve that we had been working on that might not only generate some cash, but a stronger company. We had been in conversations with one of the largest corporate travel companies in the nation about a possible merger. They were based in Boston and their business was business travel only. Ours was 70% leisure travel, so there was possibly a very strong fit for us both. All of their business was based on the east coast which was another plus because we had no franchises in the east, so we should have no competition conflicts with any of our franchisees. It could be a win – win for everyone involved. The meeting was set for Tuesday, September 28 in Boston, and we felt that it could prove productive. We were wrong.

The meetings were nonstop, hectic, and gradually turned sour. The large corporate travel company had moved from an earlier stance of a possible win – win business deal to one of trying to exploit their strength over our perceived weakness. They knew that we were now on a short financial rope and felt that we had no power to negotiate anything. After reviewing our financials and plans, and politely toying with us on Tuesday, they came directly at us Wednesday morning as an adversary. They let us know right from the start that they were only interested in taking over our programs and company for very little money. They would shut us down in Colorado and would have no use for our people. They were in the position where they thought they would just play hardball with us and see what would happen. We sat in their palatial conference room in silence while they hammered on us that we would not survive without them and there would be no further negotiations, it would be their way...take it or leave it.

We looked at each other, stood up and walked out without shaking hands or saying a word. If we were going down, then by God, it would be by our hands, not theirs.

We caught the next plane back to Denver. Upon our return, I headed to the office while our "three amigos" continued on to Seattle and the next round of meetings. As I left them at the gate we decided that this last meeting was the bad one for the week, so it was time for a good meeting with a productive outcome. It was long overdue.

The next round of meetings in Seattle did go well and Ben called me Thursday to say that things looked very good indeed.

"They are very interested in getting involved with us and realize that time is of the essence," said Ben. "I think we have two serious opportunities with this one and the L. A.

Company and I really feel that we can close them both soon. So, if Boston calls, don't even talk to them, unless you want to tell 'em to go pound sand. See you Friday morning."

As I walked toward Ben's office 7:00 a.m. Friday morning, I could hear a Jimmy Buffet song playing loudly. Ben and Ed were hard at work crunching numbers and were in great spirits. As I turned down the music so I could hear Ben, he looked up with a big grin and said, "Morning, Stevie! By the end of the day we're going to make these numbers work and by the end of next week we are going to have two commitments for money. Now crank that music back up and get out of here so we can get back to our numbers. And tell Anne to hold all calls, we don't want to be disturbed."

They worked diligently all weekend, creating various proposals for various scenarios that might come up in the meetings. The next week they would be back on the road to L.A. and then on to Seattle for more talks.

Monday morning, October 5th, Ben and Ed were off to Los Angeles to meet with the real estate company. Their CEO was back from vacation and ready to proceed with round two of negotiations. Wednesday afternoon, after two days of very productive meetings, Ben called us from the airport. I got Dave and put Ben on the speaker phone, and he announced, "Well guys, we've got a new partner. Dave, you'll get a fax with the initial documents to review in about an hour. We should be able to have everything completed by next Monday and we'll work toward a closing date of October 23. We've got to run to the gate for the Seattle flight. Talk to you tomorrow and see you Saturday morning."

Dave and I high fived each other and shouted "Great job!"

"Whoa Ben," I interrupted, "Just one question before you go. How much?"

"Oh yeah, details," Ben laughed, "$1.5 million. Gotta go."

Dave and I sat for minute in relief and then plotted our next steps. Dave would get to work on the agreement to make sure it would work, and I would get the corporate info about their company so I could start on the press releases that I would generate as soon as we could make the announcement. We not only needed the money, we needed the announcement to make to the investment community because our stock was now down to less than our original $5.00.

The week continued in a positive direction. The L.A. deal showed the capital firm in Seattle that someone else believed in us so it made it easier for them to justify their investment in us. By Friday afternoon, Ben and Ed had closed their second deal of the week. This investment would be for an initial $1 million, with the possibility of another $1 to 2 million over the next six months. We would close the deal and get the much needed funds on Friday, October 30.

Monday morning, we had an employee update meeting to make the announcements. Needless to say the news was very well received. The positive energy was once again flowing full force, as Ben told our wonderful team the well worn mantra, "The bastards won't defeat us!"

The rest of the week was spent with Ben, Dave and Ed finalizing the documents and letters of commitment, while I was busy planning a two tiered media blitz. By Friday afternoon, all the legalities were complete and the closings in place. The following Friday, October 23rd, we'd get $1.5 million from L.A., and the next Friday, October 30th, we'd get $1 million from Vancouver. By Halloween, our ghost and goblins would be gone, and it would be smooth sailing for the rest of the year.

For the first time in months, we didn't set foot in the office all weekend, we spent it celebrating with our wives and kids. It was a wonderful relaxing weekend. Our families could once again be proud of us. We refused to give up and we would not be defeated. Our lives and our company were back on track.

20

Don't You Just Hate Mondays?

Monday morning we got to the office in great spirits. This was going to be the week that got us back to full time business and once again moving forward. By the end of this week, we would have $1.5 million in working capital, and another $1 million the following week. Our short term debt would be converted to long term which would strengthen our balance sheet.

We started making phone calls to announce the good news. We were hoping that this would be the positive push that our stock needed to start the climb back up.

By the time we started calling the east coast investment companies, the stock market was off and running for the day. I either could not get through to many of the investment people, or when we did speak to them they were in a hurry to get off the phone. I kept being told that the market was acting very strange. I thought, "Yeah, whatever, but we've got important news." For the time being, they didn't seem to care.

About 9:00 a.m. I went into Ben's office to see if he was getting the same non-response.

"Yeah, it's kinda weird," said Ben "Let's go ask Mr. Stawk."

We headed down the hall to Ed's office, yanking Dave with us on the way.

"It beats me," said Ed, "There's nothing special about today. Sometimes the market will have a sell off at the end of October, but this is just a Monday and only October 19th. Let me get on the phone and see what I can find out."

Thirty minutes later, Ed was back and shaking his head in disbelief. "This is just nuts," he said quietly, "The market is in an absolute panic sell off and no one seems to know why."

Even our stock dropped a dollar, down to $4.00. This was a 20% drop in two hours. As the day wore on, we kept getting terrible updates about tremendous drops in the Dow Jones Industrial Average and NASDAQ. Each hour was much worse than the previous. It was beginning to look like a devastating high speed freeway pileup in dense fog, the wreck just kept getting bigger and bigger, with no end in sight.

When the market finally closed for the day, it was a smoldering heap of ashes. We all sat in Ben's office in a stunned silence of confused disbelief. Like hundreds of thousands of other investors and public companies, we could only wonder what had just happened to our stocks, our companies, and maybe our lives.

Tuesday morning, the Newspapers blasted the headline: BLACK MONDAY! CRASH OF 1987 ROCKS THE STOCK MARKET! Monday, October 19, 1987 was the largest stock market drop in Wall Street history. In this one ugly day, the Dow Jones Industrial Average plunged an astounding 508 points, losing 22.6% of its total value. This fall far surpassed the one-day loss of 12.9% that began the stock market crash of 1929 and foreshadowed the great depression. The plunge also triggered similar panic selling and drops in stock markets worldwide. Many stocks lost 50% of their value in this one hideous day, and billions of investors dollars vanished in thin air, never to return.

Ed was in his office on the phone to every stock analyst he knew, trying to make sense of what happened and what might happen next. Dave, Ben and I sat silently in the conference room with the TV on and the Wall Street Journal spread out in front of us. No one really knew what to say, but we were all thinking the same thing: how was this going to affect our deals that we were supposed to close this Friday and next Friday? It would take months for the market to understand what had happened and why. We didn't have time to be concerned with the why, and at this point we really didn't care. We were concerned with the one and only important priority; our survival. By the end of Black Monday, our stock dropped 40% and was now around $3.00.

Finally, Dave asked, "Well, Ben, are you going to call L.A. or are we going to wait until they call us?"

"Let's think things through before we do anything," answered Ben. We nodded in agreement. Although they were a privately held real estate company, our newest investor-to-be made much of their money through their investments in public companies. We figured that they were spinning like a top this morning, trying to calculate their own losses from Monday's explosive crash. If we didn't hear from them today, Ben would call them Wednesday morning.

Again we sat quietly, each of us lost in his own thoughts. My thoughts were of panic and survival. I couldn't stand it any longer and broke the silence, "O.K. I'll say it. Is there a chance that both investments in us could vaporize?" We just sat there, and finally Ben got up and went over to stare out the windows toward the mountains. He took a long slow breath and answered, "Yes, there's a damn good chance that both have already vaporized. Both companies may have lost the money that they were going to invest in us. Who knows how this market will shake out in the next thirty or sixty days? But we know this much; we don't have that kind of time. Guys, this might be the earthquake that we don't survive." Ben continued staring out to nowhere, perhaps staring toward the emptiness that he was feeling.

I told them that I needed to go for a walk to clear my thoughts. "Good idea," said Ben, still staring into the unknown, "If you trip over a million bucks out there, bring it back with you." I headed outside and breathed in the fresh mountain air, looking for answers. I found only elk. I thought about Ben's earthquake comment. He was right. This situation could be the one that crushes us from above or swallows us from below. We were beyond desperate with our cash flow needs, and our next payment of $800,000 as part of our purchase agreement for International Travel Partners was due on December 1st. If we missed that payment, we could forfeit the deal and the company would revert to the original owners. We had worked too hard and come too far and built too much to just have it blow up now. I wondered if there were any more aces up our sleeves that I didn't know about.

I went back to Ben's office and Ed was just heading in. I followed, thinking "Come on Ed, pull that ace out." He did not have good news. He had been tracking many of the investments held by our second investor-to-be in Seattle. Their portfolio had basically dissolved in one day. The top twelve companies that they were invested in dropped almost 60% on Monday.

"I tried calling them," Ed explained, "but naturally they are in a conference. Let's give them a few days to sort things out."

"What does your gut tell you, Ed?" I asked.

It was Ed's turn to stare out the window. "Guys, I don't think that we have a snow ball's chance in hell of getting a dime from anyone."

"Well, there's nothing we can do right now but wait," said Ben, "And hope that we can salvage one of our deals."

"There's one thing that we have to do," I replied, "Ben, you and I need to split up and talk with our employees to let them know what we know, which is basically nothing."

We meandered through the company, speaking with each employee, in small groups or one on one. We had no answers, but everyone in the company knew that we cared and would keep nothing from them.

At noon on Wednesday, we got one of the calls that we dreaded, but deep down knew was coming. The L.A. real estate company called to say that their losses were devastating and there was no way they could close on their investment. They also believed that this window of opportunity would stay closed forever. $1.5 million, poof, gone, just like that.

And then, on Friday afternoon, the Seattle call came and the other investment and hope for life died. We could have played a recording of the L.A. call, it was almost the same, word for word. This was the blow that we knew could be fatal.

At 4:30 p.m. on Friday, Ben started to call a company wide meeting to update everyone. Our promise and commitment to our employees was to keep nothing from them, but on this, I pleaded for a little time. "Ben, let's wait," I said quietly, "Nothing is going to change between now and Monday, so let's give them what may be a last peaceful weekend with their families."

Ben smiled sadly, and replied, "Yeah, you're right, and besides, maybe we can pull that last miracle this weekend." So, we let our employees head home to spend a weekend with their families and false hope.

We spent all weekend, working in denial.

We've been tossed surprise grenades over and over since we started this company and survived every one. Our credo was "The bastards won't defeat us", and with that thought cemented in our minds, we frantically searched for new ideas and pathways to survival. We stretched every possible scenario to see if there was something within that we had not yet uncovered. Ben kept going over and over our books, looking for anything liquid, or any payables that could be pushed aside to create some liquidity. After hours of hitting one brick wall after another, Ben said, "My brain's fried for the day, let's go for a drive." We hopped in Ben's Porsche, cranked up the stereo, and headed up the two lane road toward Mt. Evans. Neither us spoke as Ben pushed the 911 through its paces on the hairpin curves. On one isolated straight-away, he punched it and in an instant we were tearing along at about 130 mph. The wind ripping through our hair, the rock and roll at full blast in our ears, and a 911 at full throttle kept the world at bay, if only for a moment. Ben slowed for the next set of curves and after completing them flawlessly he stopped at an overlook. We both got out and stared toward the mountain peaks.

I picked up some rocks and pitched them toward a road sign, saying, "I'd forgotten how much fun the 911 is."

"You know what I was thinking?" asked Ben. "I was just thinking that this 911 is a whole lot like our company. It's been a great ride and gotten us to places in a hurry." He hesitated for a moment, then continued slowly and quietly, "And they'll both be gone in a few months." We looked at each other, got back in the car, and with the music off we headed back to the office at a reasonable speed in the silence of our pain.

☆☆☆☆☆☆☆☆☆☆

Monday morning we brought in all of our legal and accounting guns, and they in turn brought along their own experts. This was beyond a crisis meeting, this was a full blown conference to determine the viability of our very existence.

As the teams met for the next few days, I floated through the company, explaining to each and every person that we were fighting for our lives. It was an uphill battle, but if an answer could be found, our team would find it. My answer to everyone's question was the same - there is no answer yet. These wonderful people were actually hugging me and feeling sorry for Ben and me. They all knew that we put every penny we had into this and might lose it all. These were the most selfless and caring people that I had ever known. They came to our offices with offers to take a pay cut if it would help, and some that had the financial resources to offer to take no pay for awhile. This was their company and they were willing to fight and sacrifice for it.

The teams spent hours pouring over every number and sifting through every possible legal loophole to hold on and get through this hell.

Day by day, hour after hour into the night, they kept digging, looking, and hoping. By Wednesday evening each and every one came to the same conclusion. Any way that we crunched the numbers, they came out the same – it wasn't going to work without an infusion of cash, and there was no cash to be had.

It had been hard enough to believe that we could have found two investors before, while facing a $1.4 billion lawsuit, but trying to find a single dollar in this new market of massive losses was absolutely, undeniably, and irrevocably impossible. The party was over and we were quite simply done.

We laid out different ideas for the transition towards bankruptcy, including downsizing. We realized that downsizing would only prolong the inevitable – our demise. There was no sleep Wednesday night, knowing that Thursday morning we would begin to work out ways to make the best of a very bad and heartbreaking situation. The next few days would be the hardest of our lives.

☆☆☆☆☆☆☆☆☆

We now had only one goal, and that was the welfare of our fabulous employees. This was the finest group of human beings that I had ever known, and they had done nothing to deserve what was going to happen to them. If there was such a thing as a "right way" to proceed, we would find it.

We called an emergency EXCOM meeting for 5:00 p.m. Thursday to explain the circumstances to our managers. With their input we would develop a plan and then hold a company wide meeting on Friday, October 30 to explain the plan to everyone.

The department managers came into the conference room with a sense of foreboding. There was none of the usual joking and smiles, just solemn contemplation. Ben began to review the facts and the consequences. After thirty minutes of explanations, he explained that there was no solution other than gradually shutting down. It would take sacrifice from all of us, including immediate pay cuts, and we wanted each manager's thoughts as to the best way to help our employees through this ordeal.

My mom used to say that the best of times bring nothing but joy, but the worst of times brings out the best in good people, and the worst in bad people.

Stan Radtke stood up and started pacing back and forth. Ben asked, "Stan, any thoughts?"

"Yeah, can the fat chicks and the old ones first," Stan blurted out.

I never liked this guy, but didn't know why until now. The room full of people with character and honor just stared at this jerk in disbelief.

Ben said, "Stan, I'm going to forget you said that. I suggest that you sit down."

"I don't think so, Ben, you asked for my input and now you're going to get it," responded Stan.

"Sacrifices? Look, just because you guys screwed this thing up, don't tell me about sacrifices for the employees. They're employees, screw them, better yet get rid of them. I made my sacrifice when I left a major cruise line to come here on your promises. You expect me to take a pay cut for them? I don't think so. As a matter of fact, I'm supposed to get a year end bonus and my wife expects a big Christmas."

No one in the room could believe what they were hearing. My heart started racing and I could feel the blood pounding in my head. I took his remarks absolutely personal, because these people were like family and God love 'em, they were what made our company. I swear that if I had a gun I would have pulled the trigger.

I exploded and yelled, "Stan, you are a pompous, arrogant, egotistical self-serving asshole. I really don't know how you became part of this company."

"Sure, I'm an asshole, but you know what? Bill brought me in here to build the cruise department and I'm the leader that got the job done. Why do you think the cruise convention with those idiot travel agents was so successful? Me, that's why."

"So let me be brutally honest for all of you. It's not about them, it's about us, here in this room, and how we can survive. Outside this room are a bunch of employees, they come and go, and they're a dime a dozen. Yeah, you bet it's me first, and foremost. That's why I'm a leader."

"And you know what else, Steve, if that makes

me an asshole, so be it."

His attack on these people who were the very fiber of our company was the final straw. I had to get out of this room before I flew across the table. I stood up and walking to the door, took a deep breath and said, "I have to get away from this negativity. Stan, you're like a cancer. It's losers like you that will destroy great people and a good company. Our mission here to find the most positive approach to our employees' futures, not listen to you whine." Staring straight at Ben and Bill, I continued, "Bill, this fool reports to you, and Ben, Bill reports to you. I suggest that you two figure something out so we can resume this critical meeting in a positive manner. I need to take a break." This guy was the Grand Canyon of assholes and I felt if I spent another minute around him I'd earn an honorary degree in Proctology.

I started out the door and Bill Lever stopped me. He sadly shook his head and pointed his shaking finger at Stan. Bill was ten years older than me and much wiser. I respected him greatly and waited for him to speak.

Almost in a whisper, he began. "Steve, please let me apologize to you, and everyone in this room. Stan, I am very disappointed in you. You are a disgrace upon me and to this wonderful company. Let me make this very clear to you, Stan, you are not a leader, you never were and you never will be. I've heard it said that a manager does things right, but a leader does the right things. When you leave this room, there will be no one here but leaders, people that care about people, and about doing the right things. Please go to my office now."

"No," said Ben. "Let's take a fifteen minute break. Stan and Bill, you both come with me to my office."

Twenty minutes later, Ben and Bill returned to the conference room to explain that Stan had turned in his resignation. The first and only justified downsizing in our company's history had just taken place. There was no discussion about it, there didn't need to be. We got back to our one purpose, to make tomorrow's meeting as positive as possible. We were all in this together, and unlike Stan, no one had to be reminded that ethics are not situational, they are real and constant, and simply part of us all.

21

Pushing Water Uphill With A Rake

F riday afternoon, we gathered all of the employees into the reservation center for the hardest and saddest meeting of our lives.

We spent nearly an hour explaining the full details and circumstances, and most of the employees could tell where the story was leading. Tissues appeared as eyes started to swell with tears. We explained that we had examined every conceivable possibility to stay in business and we came up with no solutions, because there were none.

Several people began to cry. All sat in total shock, disbelief and denial. The questions of sheer panic started flying toward us.

"But you guys can find a solution, you always find solutions!"

"This can't be real. We've come too far and done too much to give up now."

"What if we take half our salary? What if we can afford to take none for a month?"

"There's got to be money out there."

"We can't just give up."

"What about this? Why don't we try that?"

"How about calling"…and it continued on and on and on and on, until all the ideas and tears were drained. We fully expected this reaction because we knew the goodness of these people. There was very little anger, no bitterness, just immense pain, sorrow and heartbreak. This company was a living and loving entity and these people were its heart and blood flow, and by God, they were not going down without a gallant effort to survive.

We answered each question and let them work out their thoughts and feelings. Now it was time to continue with the beginning of the end. I took a long slow breath and began the most disheartening statement of my life.

"Look, my friends, this is it. We have examined it all and we have tried everything, but this is like trying to push water uphill with a rake. You may work hard at it, but it can't be done. It's absolutely over. Our company is dead."

It was if I had just flipped the switch on a giant exhaust fan. My words sucked the energy, the hope, and the hearts from the room. All that was left were tears and stunned grief. I gave them a moment then handed the meeting to Ben.

"Please listen to me carefully, this is very important. You are all incredibly talented professionals and wonderful people. Our company will not survive, but all of you will – somewhere else."

Eyes began to look up and toward Ben as he continued.

"We will pay you as long as possible. Right now, I don't know how long that will be. Tonight, you're going to go home in shock, and have a real crummy weekend. But Monday we want you back in here bright and early, because as of Monday we are your outsourcing company. We will get everyone's resume out, dust it off, and update and polish it. Each of you has grown immensely and your new resumes will reflect that. We will sit with each of you to see what company or industry that you would like to go to, and we'll start the phones and meetings to make sure that you have the best possible jobs as soon as possible. You'll get together in teams and role play interviews. We'll use our phones, faxes, computers, supplies, and contacts to get you the type of jobs you deserve. You are great assets to any company and you will all move on to better things."

"No Ben," said one of our managers, "I know that I speak for everyone when I say that we all know that none of us will go on to better things, 'cause this is as good as it gets."

"Thanks," said Ben, "Then we'll see each and every one of you on Monday."

They filed out of the office like mourners leaving the funeral of a loved one. Each headed home to a weekend of worry, wondering what and where their future would be.

☆☆☆☆☆☆☆☆☆☆

Saturday, our department managers came in and began pulling all the resumes out of the files. Each manager laid the resumes out in front of them and spent the day adding strong comments to each.

Meanwhile, Ben and I were meeting with our personal accountant and attorney. We had to sort out the magnitude of our personal losses. It was actually quite easy; we had lost everything we had. We had spent all of our money building the company to the point of going public, and took only small salaries after that. Tom, our attorney pointed out that we had personally guaranteed asset purchases like the $250,000 mainframe computer, the $75,000 copy machine, phone system, etc.

"Guys, let's review the ugly facts," said Tom, "Many of the corporate losses will attach to you personally. The $1.4 billion lawsuit, if ever successful in some form, will attach itself to you. You may also be open to all sorts of anger lawsuits from investors or even employees. You both have mortgages on your homes in excess of 120%." Before he could continue, Ben interrupted.

"Oh sure, try to cheer us up", Ben quipped, "Look, Steve and I know the details and we know the outcome, we just need you to confirm it."

"O.K., here's the bottom line. You, my friends, are flat out, dead broke and you both will have to start planning to file personal bankruptcy for two reasons. One, you're actually bankrupt. Two, bankruptcy is the only protection you and your families have to start over from scratch and begin the slow process of building a new life."

Whew, these words really hit home. Like Ben said, he and I knew the facts and the diagnosis, but it felt like the doctor telling you that you have a terminal disease. When Tom said it out loud, it was irrefutable and it lay heavily on us both. Ben and I both grew up in small Midwestern towns where things like this didn't happen. Bankruptcy was a personal disgrace, the scarlet letter B, and you might as well have it branded on your forehead.

Tom looked at us both and noticed our reaction. "Ben, Steve, listen to me. This happened because both of you committed everything to building something of great value for a lot of people. You played the risk - return ratio game like the true entrepreneurs that you are. You were an inch away from millions and now you're an inch away from poverty. Yes, you'll have to file bankruptcy, and yes, you'll lose all your assets including your houses, and yes, you'll have to start your lives over. But, guys, this doesn't define either of you as people, it is just something terrible that happened to you. Please don't let it eat at you personally because it will hold you back from your future."

Ben and I both shuddered, then shook off the meeting; we'd have to think about it later, because right now we had to take care of our employees as best we could.

✩✩✩✩✩✩✩✩✩✩

We spent the rest of the day working with our managers, going over resumes. Each resume we reviewed was like looking at our family album, and we sat around telling "remember when" stories like a couple of proud parents.

By the end of the day, I was emotionally exhausted and physically drained from this past week. Now it was time to go home and try to explain everything to my own family, but it was all too real and painful to discuss. Throwing all of this at Laura and the kids would serve no purpose now because there were still too many things that I had to sort out. There was no reason to let the concerns start to wear on them, there would be plenty of time for that later. Facing our employees with this huge failure was crushing, but it would pale in comparison to the failure that I was going to inflict upon my wife and kids. For now, this was the meeting that I was not capable of having, and my family was the one group that I could not yet face.

22

The Worthless Knight In Rusted Armor

At the final bell, the greatest accomplishment a man can have is the love and respect of his family, and I was very lucky to have a wonderful wife and kids. When I first met her at a teen dance, Laura was all of fifteen, and I was a manly sixteen. By the end of the summer I knew that I loved her. We grew up together, got married while in college, and had our kids while still kids ourselves. Many people wondered, as we did sometimes, why we were together, because we really had very little in common. I lived for and thrived off of people; talking to people, working with people, developing people, just being around people – the more the merrier. I also loved business; creating, building and being a part of business. I was the total extrovert.

Laura was the total opposite. She was a stay at home introvert, and a voracious reader. In my social activities, I could discuss books because Laura was my living Cliff Notes to the world of literature. Corporate social functions were as much fun for her as root canal surgery and she often came across as an acerbic non-conversationalist. The few lucky ones that got to know her realized that she just had no use for either chit or his sister, chat.

She was also mistakenly placed in this century. We often joked that her real name was Laura Ingalls and she was living in a Twilight Zone episode where she was snatched from her 19th century little house on the prairie and thrust into this strange 20th century place. When she read the Foxfire books, it was like reading her own journal.

Laura was a very good person that, quite honestly, had no particular use for the human race as a species. She loved the land, nature and all animals, the more she had, the happier she was. When we moved to Colorado and I immersed myself in business, she finally got the horses that she had wanted her whole life, and spent hours grooming and riding them.

She also became a pillar in the mountain animal protective league. Over the years, she fostered over one hundred dogs that had been dumped in the mountains. Because of her, each one was adopted, not one was euthanized.

Our commonality was our love and our respect for each other, and our love, adoration, and total devotion to our kids. Our differences and opposites created a strong balance for raising them. Together, we were this strange and strong partnership that built a wonderful loving, laughing and caring family.

Because of my prior success, we had a lovely mountain home. We couldn't see our nearest neighbor, which was just fine for Laura, and it was full of animals. We had horses, dogs, cats, assorted gerbils and rabbits, and my daughter's pet miniature donkey, Yankee (he was born on the 4th of July, so his full name was Yankee Doodle Donkey). In addition to our menagerie, there were always the foster dogs, being trained by Laura to be adoptable by permanent homes.

In the busy frantic pace that I lived and thrived on, it was our home, and Laura and the kids that kept me balanced and grounded. Whenever I got too full of myself, (which was probably much too often) Laura would yank me back to reality. Unloading hay, repairing fences, cleaning the barn, going on trail rides and playing with my family recharged my batteries for that other life.

Ours was a wonderful life, and I was extremely proud that I had been able to provide such a life for my family. I always had a warm glow of satisfaction inside, knowing that they were all very proud of me.

But now it was all changing.

As an entrepreneur, I had risked everything that we had to create an even better life for us, and I now knew that I was going to lose it all, and I wondered if I would be able to keep my family intact.

I'm no psychologist, but I deeply believe that in my generation there a vast difference between men and women when it comes to a failure like this. I was like most baby boomer men, raised like our fathers before us; that there is an unspoken duty and purpose in life for a man to provide well for his family. This is not just what we *do*, but who and what we *are*. It is our purpose in life, and earns us love and respect.

I believe that the main desired accomplishment for a man, whether he admits it or not, is to know that he is respected by his family and peers. Not a respect from power, but rather a respect that has been earned through hard work, sacrifice, and accomplishments that build a quality life and peaceful security for those that he loves. My fulfillment and complacency came from knowing that my family was proud of me.

Men want and need to be the knight in shining armor for their family. We must be, and take great pride in being, the strong provider and protector. I also think that a man's wife and family want to think of him that way.

I found that when this failure hit home, I faced a pain and total sense of worthlessness that I would not have believed could exist. I cannot, to this day, find words that can aptly describe the emptiness, hopelessness, confusion, heartbreak, and sense of losing oneself that I was experiencing.

I had no idea what I was thinking or feeling because this was all new (excuse me, Professor, but there were no chapters about this in my business books).

Here I was, this thirty six year old guy, married seventeen years to a wonderful woman with our two great teenagers, and I had always taken care of them. I know of nothing else that can be more humiliating to a man than not being able to provide for his family. Now, instead of a provider, I was trying to figure out how to be a survivor.

Day by day and week by week I slipped into a deeper psychological abyss. It was a very dark and surreal existence of no longer knowing who I was, wondering what happened to the Other Steve, the Knowing Steve, the Good Steve. I hated this new person that had become this worthless knight in rusted armor that was destroying his family's life.

As a man of strength, this was not something that I could discuss with other men. It's a guy thing. Men discuss success with other men, not failure. Our misguided pride does not allow this type of dialog. Discussing failure is discussing weakness, and real men are not supposed to be weak. And this was certainly not anything that I could discuss with the wife who trusted me to have solutions, not unknown problems without solutions.

So I fell into the trap of talking only to myself and trying to think things out only with myself. This is a huge mistake when one is living in depression. I was sharing one dimensional thinking with a nonobjective person – me. The negative was overtaking the positive and feeding on itself.

I knew that we were not going to come

through this with our home and other assets. I had leveraged them and lost them all, and it was only a matter of time before they would be reclaimed. How was I going to tell my family that I had failed them and that we were going to lose our home? How would I tell my daughter that she would have to give Yankee to a new home? How could I tell Laura that her horses would be sold? Our animals were living members of our family and she loved them dearly.

I was holding out any hope against hope that some miracle might fall from the sky, and until I was certain that there were no good answers, I could not discuss anything.

So I created a cold and painful relationship of avoidance.

Laura was also lost and confused. She was constantly uncertain of what was going on because I could not or would not communicate. What could I say? I was trying to figure out if there was a way to get through this hell, but all I knew so far was that the light at the end of the tunnel was an oncoming train. I had been the one that always figured things out and now I had no answers, so I went to great lengths to avoid her questions. I was at the office seven days a week anyway, but I would try to not get home until close to bedtime to avoid conversation. We kept conversation around our kids, and left it at that.

I wouldn't open, or get involved in other discussions for fear of where it would lead. I already hated myself for letting everyone down, from our fantastic employees to my precious family. I simply couldn't handle the thought of Laura no longer having any faith in me, and probably losing her love for me. I had created an environment that only fed the confusion and helpless feeling between us. When I caught a glance from her I withered inside. From her glance, she was wondering why I was angry at her and why I didn't want anything to do with her. But when I saw the glance, I read it to mean that she was glancing in contempt at this hideous loser that had let her family down.

When she would attempt to open a dialog by trying to say something to comfort me, in my twisted mind it felt like pity, which cut me even deeper. One doesn't pity a strong man, one pities the weak and pathetic, and that must be what she was really thinking.

So our relationship of avoidance continued, creating a no-win self-feeding fire that was destroying our marriage.

As the weeks wore on, my despair and silent depression grew and magnified in ways that I never thought possible. My self esteem had vanished, replaced with self doubt. I wondered over and over if I really had any brains or talent, or had all of this just been a lucky fluke? And if it was just luck, was this my one and only chance that would never occur again? I would not have the financial means to start another company, and who in their right mind would want to hire an independent loser like me? Sure,

I had accomplished some good thing, but sometimes the good that you do doesn't do you any good.

I next crossed into a fight or flight mode. But who was there to fight? The enemy of my family was me, and how do I fight me? As for flight, you bet I wanted to flee all of this. In my state of mind, I had reached the point were my new four letter word in life was *responsibility*, and God, how I hated it. I had been working since age nine, always responsible. I worked my way through college with a wife and babies and always strived to take care of others. I now hated responsibility and cursed it!

My heart moved out of the way and my deluded mind and broken spirit took over. Ever since I was a kid, I lived with the motto, "If it's to be, it's up to me". When I wanted my new bike, a 26" black Schwinn Spitfire with gold pin striping, I worked, saved and bought that bike; and my Yamaha Big Bear '360 motorcycle, and yes, my black two door, hard top '57 Chevy packing a 327 four barrel carburetor. Yeah, it was the same with college, and on and on, yada, yada, blah blah blah, ad nausea.

Oh yeah, sure, "If it's to be, it's up to me". What a load of crap.

So, now what about ME?

Maybe I don't want IT to be.

What if I just don't want anything to be up to ME?

I was absolutely sick and tired of *anything* being up to ME!

I was struck with this bolt of lightning that declared to the world that I DON'T want a wife and I DON'T want these kids and I DON'T want this big house and all those animals and all the responsibility that goes with all of it! I DON'T want a damn company and damned employees. I DON'T want any of it and I sure as hell don't need it. To Hell with 'em all! I could easily survive on my own. I'd run away and be a bartender in a bar in the Caribbean. I'd work when I wanted to, or just lay in a hammock with a cold drink, without a thought about anyone or anything. Yep, I'd just leave everything far behind and forget about it all.

These thoughts lasted about two weeks, then wore themselves out. I gave up on the concept because I was too damn responsible and I knew it. All the responsibility, and the junk that comes with it, was the very definition of me, and I could not change it if I wanted to. I couldn't even be a good bum.

It's been said that success has many fathers, while failure is an orphan. But there was no escaping the fact that this failure was my baby and it was destroying those around me.

I finally came to realize that I had become the ultimate failure. I sincerely felt for the first time in my life that I was of no real value to anyone and was more valuable to my family dead than I was alive. As part of our management benefit package, Ben and I had million dollar life insurance policies paid for by the company. I was not worth two cents alive, but my family would have $1 million if I was dead. I could not save my wonderful family, but my life insurance could. For weeks, I silently and very seriously contemplated suicide. I went to Kmart and looked at guns, but I decided that a violent death would not be fair to Laura and the kids. I thought over every possible scenario and turned each one down because of the psychological consequences to others. Hell, I was even a failure at getting rid of the only problem in my family's life – me.

I finally settled on a sound plan. I would take my camera and drive up the road toward Mt. Evans. Along the road were several pull offs with trails that lead back to huge boulders and cliffs that overlook five hundred foot drop-offs. I would take some pictures from the edge, before going over with my camera. It would be a tragic, clumsy accidental death, just like my life. My wife and family would be taken care of, my kids would go to college. Who said I had no answers? Problem solved.

I only had to work out the timing. There were still those good old responsibilities that had to be taken care of before I could take the final solution. I still had to make sure that the rest of our employees had good jobs to go to. Most of the people had moved on, but we still had about twenty with us.

☆☆☆☆☆☆☆☆☆☆

It was now the last week of November. We had

faked our way through Thanksgiving and were headed toward a non-Christmas. Each day was spent winding down more things at the office; taking the still constant phone calls, saying goodbye to more employees, and gradually putting the company to death.

Friday afternoon, Mel came into to my office with a worried look, "Steve, I just spoke to your dad while you were on the conference call. Please call him right away. It's your mom."

My heart raced as I punched the numbers, Dad answered on the first ring. I could tell in his voice that something was terribly wrong.

"Dad, what is it? Is Mom O.K.?"

"Steve, I just got back from the hospital. Your mom has another brain tumor, and I afraid that this one is inoperable." The words literally sucked the air from me. I got dizzy and thought I would pass out. This could not be happening, not now, not ever. Mom had several battles with cancer over the years and fought them all. She had survived breast cancer and mastectomies twice, and then three years ago she had a brain tumor removed. The tumor had been declared benign, and we thought that we were out of the woods.

Dad explained that several months ago she started losing her balance occasionally, and then the headaches started. Finally they went back to the specialist. Tests showed that either a piece of the old tumor had remained or a new one developed. Their best guess was that it was probably malignant. Because of the size and location of the tumor, coupled with Mom's age and ill health, the surgeons determined that her chances of living through any surgery were very slim to none.

"Dad, what does all that mean?" I was pleading for some kind of assurance that things would be alright.

My dad broke down and sobbed, "Steve, they think that your mom has six to eight weeks left."

I couldn't speak. I couldn't move. I couldn't breath. I could feel my blood rushing through my head and I thought that the pressure was going to explode my ears. Finally the words came out, "Dad, I'm on my way. I'll call you when I make my flight arrangements."

I ran to Ben's office to fill him in and grabbed a book of flight passes that we still had. Ben had Mel start checking flights while I drove home to pack and tell Laura and the kids. Three hours later I was on a flight to Houston to connect with a flight to Orlando. For the first time in months, I was not consumed with corporate and personal problems. They didn't matter for now. After takeoff I spent the next several hours thinking only of Mom.

I'm proud to tell anyone who even appears to be listening that my mom was, without question, the best mom in the world. She was this incredibly positive person that saw the goodness in everyone and believed in the potential of each. She had this wonderful sense of humor and caring, not just for her three sons, but with everyone that she knew. I got my good

old German work ethic from my dad, and my
creativity, love of people, and Irish sense of
humor from Mom. She was always there for us
with unconditional love and support.

I landed in Orlando at midnight, rented a car
and headed for the hospital in Daytona Beach.
By 2:00 a.m. I was at Mom's side, and stayed
with her until sunrise, then drove to Dad's condo
to console him and grab a quick shower. We
were back at the hospital by 9:00 a.m. and
stayed until we were asked to leave. Dad and I
went to dinner and back to the condo and talked
into the night. Sunday morning it was back to
the hospital with a break for lunch and dinner.
Monday morning I left Daytona at 5:00 a.m. to
get back to the Orlando airport and make it back
to the office by 2:00 p.m.

I repeated this nonstop routine for the next
few weeks; a long tedious week at the office,
straight to the airport, drive to the hospital,
Mom, Dad, back to the office on Monday. I
wasn't sleeping at home or on the road. I was in
this constant surreal existence of watching my
company gradually die, followed by watching
Mom, this incredibly precious gift from God,
also gradually die. Over and over, never ending,
it was taking its toll. I was numb to everyone and
everything around me. I remember watching an
interview with Mother Theresa where she said,
"God never gives us more than he thinks that we
can take, but there have been times when I
wished that he didn't have quite so much trust in
me." I was about a million miles from a Mother

Theresa, but I kept thinking, "Will someone please just stop this ride so I can get off? I'm really going to be sick!"

One weekend while sitting with Mom, she was actually feeling pretty well and we talked for hours. We went over stories of growing up, the mischief that three boys got into, and her questions about her beloved grandkids. She asked about the company and some of the employees that she had come to know, and without me realizing it, my tone changed. Typically Mom, she read me like a comic book. "My, so serious", she said. "Smile for me, life is too serious to take seriously." She asked if something was wrong and I denied everything. Mom held my hand, looked at me, smiling and said, "Whatever it is Honey, I'm sure you'll figure it out. You always have since you were a little boy. Like you've always said, "If it's to be, it's up to me."

I smiled back and assured her that she was right, and changed the subject back to her grandkids. As I said before, she was the world's best mom, but that was just practice to become the best grandma in the entire universe. Her grandkids absolutely loved and adored her. We talked and laughed about the kids for another hour until she was worn out.

Monday morning, I was on the plane, heading back to my other wake-in-waiting. The flight back was spent in fond thoughts and memories of simpler happy times growing up in Indiana with my mom to care for me. I longed to return to those days, but it was not going to happen. What was going to happen was my life here, now, and in the future. As I reflected on life with Mom and then the current circumstances in my life, I had my first attack of logic in months. Watching my precious mother slip away was actually putting other things in my life in perspective.

Two important thoughts finally emerged from my battered brain. One was my own credo, "Know yourself, trust yourself, believe in yourself, then get over yourself." I finally began to realize that as bad as everything was, others have things worse. The second was, as Mom reminded me, "If it's to be, it's up to me." As always, Mom knew best. It was then that I knew that I was in this life to take whatever it threw me, and in spite of my prior "solution" I would not give up the fight.

☆☆☆☆☆☆☆☆☆☆

I got back to the office around 2:30 Monday afternoon, and as I was sorting through my pile of messages, Laura called. "Steve, I know that you're slammed, but please come home early. We need to talk." I felt like a kid being called to the principal's office. I knew we needed to talk, that we *had* to talk, but I still didn't know how, or what to say. But I knew it was time and it was important. For the first time in months, I went home at 5:00 p.m. It was holiday break and the kids were staying all night with friends, so we had an empty kitchen to fill with conversation. We sat at the kitchen table, looking at each other in silence. Finally, Laura took a slow breath and began, "This weekend while you were gone, our daughter asked if we were getting divorced." She could see the shock on my face, which only increased when she continued, "I told her the truth; that I didn't know."

Before I could respond, she went on, "Look Steve, for whatever strange and unexplainable reason, other than our love for each other, we are partners in this life. I know that these are terrible times for you, but I thought that we were always a team and in this together, but you've totally shut us out. You must believe that I see the pain grow in you every day, but you won't let me in to help. We hurt with you and for you, but by keeping us away you are hurting the three of us, and it's just not right."

I sat motionless. I tried to speak, but the words were stuck in my heart. She was absolutely correct, but she didn't realize that in my state of depression and exhaustion, I was incapable of offering comment.

"I know you're heartbroken over the company, we all are. And of course you're devastated about Mom. But guess what, it's not just you, it's all of us. Steve, please listen carefully to what I'm going to say."

"Your mother is dying. We are going to lose her, it rips our hearts out, but it's going to happen and there is nothing that we can do about it."

"The company that you have put your life into is dying. I know it's like a family to you, and that it's breaking your heart to go through it, and it breaks my heart watching you. But it's going to happen and there is nothing that you can do about it."

"But you are also very close to losing your real family, the wife and kids that love you dearly. This is the one loss that you and only you can prevent. Before long everything else in your life that you care about will be gone, it's up to you to decide if our family will survive. You have to decide if you want us." This loving woman finally broke through the steel wall that I had built between us.

"You're absolutely right", I answered, "I've kept you all out and it was wrong. And yes, I want us. It may take all night, but I'll tell you everything. But when you know the totality, you may not want me."

With that, I began talking, and once I started, it spilled out for hours. I explained the circumstances and dire consequences, including the fact that we would lose our house and home. It was painful and shocking but we discussed our future and how we would work through things together. Together – that word had a great ring to it. After hours of painful discussions, our dialog gradually returned to the way it used to be – the way it should be. We even found some things to laugh about in the midst of the gloom. We talked and talked until we were both exhausted. I felt so much better getting everything off my chest, but still felt immense guilt for what I was putting us through.

I had to say one final thing, "I have failed all of you and I have ruined our lives and I am very sorry. Laura, if you want to call it quits and take the kids and leave me, I understand."

She stood up, leaned over the table and stared into my eyes and said, "Let me get this straight, we're going to lose everything so I'll divorce you and take the kids and, let's see…oh, yeah, 50% of NOTHING? Steve I've known you since I was fifteen, we've grown up together and I know you better than anyone. So you blew it big and you lost everything, but I believe in you and I know that some day you'll get it all back." She sat back down, and with a grin, added, "Then we'll talk." We laughed and for the first time in months, we were once again *us*.

Here I was, this guy who was supposedly the strong one in the family, drawing this incredible strength from the women in my life, my wife and my mom. It took me thirty six years and a major life crisis to discover the quiet, constant, and invincible strength of women that love their families. It took thirty six years too long to learn this obvious truth, but I was happy to finally get the wake up call. The next day, I stayed home and we explained everything to our fantastic kids. Life was back to the four us and somehow we'd get through this together.

23

Arranging The Deck Chairs

I t was now January and our shut down was progressing toward the end. Ed moved on to a large regional stock firm as head analyst, and later became president. Dave joined the National Association of Securities Dealers as a top litigator, and then moved on to private practice, and Bill Lever went back to the cruise industry that he knew so well, and later became president of a large cruise line. And, without exception, each of our valuable employees found new and worthwhile jobs.

Every day was made of hugs, tears and goodbyes as we watched these fine people moving on to new lives. We each have our own ways of grieving and disguising feelings and pain. There's no right or wrong, it just is what it is. Ben came from a military family and was not open to expressions of affection or feelings as our employees left. He kept his feelings inside and basically tried to ignore people as they left. I knew Ben well and knew that it was simply too hard to say goodbye over and over, because each goodbye was an acknowledgment of guilt for this failure. The one thing that he had left was his military type pride. Occasionally when people would stop by to say farewell, Ben would pick up the phone as if he were on a call and just wave goodbye to them. He would then watch from the window as they drove away and comment, "Well, there goes another one, jumping ship."

"Yeah, those selfish bastards", I'd answer in my most sarcastic voice. "How dare they go on to their new lives, just because we told them to. How could they possibly leave, when they could stay here with the captain on the Titanic and arrange the deck chairs until we all go under." Ben would look at me, and a small grin would appear as he rather impolitely suggested that I go somewhere very warm and have sex with myself.

The last group to go had stayed to help us shut things down while they waiting to start their new jobs. We had no money to pay them, but we had furniture, so we said, "Do you like your office? Then take your office. Didn't you always love that picture? Then take the picture." It was the only way that we could compensate them but it helped. We also used the furniture to pay many of our smaller local vendors in lieu of money.

☆☆☆☆☆☆☆☆☆☆

I also began the tedious process of filing for personal bankruptcy. I learned once again that as you go through failure, your values are always being tested. The first bankruptcy attorney that I met with explained the procedure. First, I'd have to pay him $2,500 in advance. This meant that I would have to save the money and get back to him, because you can't file bankruptcy if you're broke (go figure).

He blew me away with his next bit of sage advice. He asked if I had any credit cards with credit remaining on them. I replied yes, and he told me to "Do something nice for your family". He suggested that I take them on a shopping spree, like at Christmas. Then we'd just write it off with the other debts.

I said, "Wait a minute, let me get this straight. You're telling me to use my remaining credit to purchase things, with absolutely no intention of paying for them in the future?"

"Yes", he replied, "That's how the system works. These big companies don't give a damn about you and they just write it off, so think of your family and do something nice for them."

I must admit that I sat there, thinking about what I was putting my family through. Maybe this guy was right, this would be a nice gift for them to help lessen the pain that I was inflicting on them. And this is how the "system works". I told him that I'd think about it.

On the drive home, I tried my best to justify what he had told me, "Think of my family, think of my family". I decided that he was right. The world had screwed me over so the hell with them. I went to bed agreeing with him, I would do something nice for my family.

At 3:00 a.m., I awoke and lay staring at the ceiling. My heart was racing and my stomach was on fire. I knew that I could not even think about following this guy's advice. I was no attorney but I knew that when you "buy" something with no intention of paying for it, it's not "playing the system", it's just plain stealing. I loved my family and wanted to lighten their load but this was just wrong. They were smart people and when they used the credit cards, would quickly understand what was happening, which would make them accessories to this crime of "playing the system." I had already lost most of my stuff, but I could not teach my kids that when times get tough they can set aside their honesty. I was determined that I would not give up my honesty or integrity, for my kids sake as well as my own. The next day, I called the jerk and told him that I would not use him, and why. His reply was a flippant "Fine, it's your loss."

☆☆☆☆☆☆☆☆☆

By the end of January, it was finally down to just Ben and me. All of the offices were empty and dark except for ours. We had stayed as long as possible to use the office to try to get on with our own futures, but time was out and it was the last week before the locks would be changed.

I finished packing up my files, and went to Ben's office to see how I could help him. He was sitting on the couch in his office, sipping a drink and staring into the past. He pointed to a half full bottle of Jack Daniels on his desk and invited me to join him. I topped Ben's drink off and poured myself one, and sat down beside Ben with the bottle between us. We sat sipping Jack in silence, both looking at the boxes and stacks of files waiting to be packed, and wondering what had happened to our company and our lives.

Out of nowhere, Ben said, "You know I lost a lot more than you did."

I didn't look at Ben, I just stared straight ahead, wondering where this was coming from. I assumed that this was just Ben's frustration coming out. It was true that Ben had more money to put into the company than I did, and he had more personal assets that he was going to lose. But whatever the amount, when you lose everything it still adds up to *every thing*.

After awhile I replied, "Damn, Ben, nobody told me it was going to be a competition. You're right, you had more to lose and you lost more. Congratulations, you win! I guess I just didn't try hard enough, but if we ever do this again, I'll do my best to lose more than you and I promise to definitely lose more than 100%."

Again, silence, and then we looked at each other and burst out laughing. We clinked glasses and Ben said, "Sorry Steve, but you know I'm way too competitive to let you beat me at anything, least of all at losing money. Nope, I'll always lose more than you." We started laughing, almost hysterically for several minutes, releasing months of pent up emotions. I guess it was as close to breaking down in tears and hugs that we could get.

After we settled down, I raised my glass to Ben, "Here's to one hell of a ride." We toasted and got back to work, boxing up our lives. At the end of the month, Ben and I moved in different directions to different lives, always staying friends.

☆☆☆☆☆☆☆☆☆☆

Three years later, I got a phone call from Dave. He had just received notification that the $1.4 Billion lawsuit had finally made it to court and it had been promptly dismissed as a suit without merit.

"Congratulations, we won", sighed Dave.

Yeah, we won. Whoopee, what a victory! One tiny battle, too little and too late. The action that spun our company and our lives into ruin was finally proven to be without merit. Though it was perhaps justice, I got no satisfaction when Dave further explained that the two agencies who sued us had also filed for bankruptcy. It was all for nothing, and I had hollow burning inside as I allowed myself to start thinking "what if?" But you can "what if" yourself into depression and slow down forward progress, so I tried to put it aside and go on with my new life.

As we go through life, we all have some memories in our past that hurt deeply. But these were not memories of the past, except for the end, those memories were wonderful. I know that this may sound strange, but what hurt more were the *memories of the future*...the memories of what *could* have been, what *should* have been, but what was *never to be*.

As the years went by, I took even more pride in the wonderful group of people that had been part of this dream. I would occasionally run into some of our former employees and always got the same response; a big hug and the statement, "It was the absolute best, and we were so close." I held a deep satisfaction in knowing that these wonderful people had moved on to bright futures, and took comfort and pride in knowing that we did all that we could to help them get there.

Yes, it had been one hell of a ride. We had created something from nothing and done things that had never been done before, and we could take great pride in that. We also took pride in the fact that we did our very best for our employees. Ben and I lost our company, our money, our homes and personal assets. We were by no means martyrs, just two guys trying to do something big, and trying to do it right.

I had lost my corporate family, but somehow I kept my real family together through shattered dreams and the worst of times. In times of immense failure, perhaps this was my success. I didn't have a clue what I would do with the rest of my life, but I realized now that if it's to be, it really *is* up to me. It would be difficult, but I would never stop trying and never give up on my dreams. I still had an absolute passion for business and a lust for life and I would not give up on either. I would not only survive, I would succeed.

Epilogue

When it comes to starting a business in this great nation of ours, I have good news and bad news:

The good news is that 98% of all businesses in the United States are small businesses. This certainly bodes well for the independent spirit and entrepreneurial drive that have made our country great.

The bad news is that 80% new businesses will fail within the first five years. That's right, a full eight out of ten will be gone within five years.

I firmly believe that the freedom for anyone to engage in the quest for success is what makes America the great and strong nation that it is. But free enterprise, like our cherished freedom, is not necessarily free. The pursuit of free enterprise comes with great responsibility. Business leaders must accept responsibility for their actions, as well as the ethical obligation to "do the right thing" with their customers, their investors, and, most of all, their employees.

American business ethics should not be an oxymoron. There is no such thing as "situational ethics." Ethics should be real and constant in business, as well as in life.

The big companies get the big press, but all

business failures, large and small, can have devastating effects on the lives of those involved. Almost daily, there's another story about corporate corruption and business failures in America. With every story, I get more and more angry. My anger is ignited by the lowlife weasels who believe they have a right to blunder and plunder their way through a company for their own personal gain. What is most infuriating is the cause and effect on honest, hardworking people who have had their futures stolen and their lives destroyed.

The real disaster behind a business failure is the "trickle down failure," and it is attacking the boomer generation the hardest. As a consequence of business failures and ongoing downsizings, men and women in their mid-forties and fifties are faced with a new career search that is leading nowhere. They are "overqualified" and will be passed over for younger employees willing to work for less.

The hard truth is that many will never regain the same status or income level, while many others will face financial ruin. As you are reading this, Americans are filing personal bankruptcy at a new record pace. Too many of these are people who have been in control of their lives but are now waking up to a different life, one that doesn't make sense. Their new financial stress and burden to survive will often create a serious challenge to personal ethics, honesty, and integrity.

I often speak to business groups and civic

organizations, and after many of my speaking engagements, I am asked about the status of my marriage. More often than not, the people asking the question confess that they went through a financial failure and then experienced a breakup in their marriage or relationship. Unfortunately, one major consequence of financial failure is the psychological pain of being unable to provide for one's family. I experienced first hand how this distress shuts down communication and creates new levels of stress that can destroy relationships. I was one of the lucky ones that made it through. Many do not.

Through our pains in life, we can gain knowledge. It's said that a quality education is expensive. Well, you could say that I paid for a PhD in life and I learned some valuable lessons.

I learned the hard way that everyone can fail when they do things wrong, but guess what? You can also do everything *right* and still fail. But as tough as it is, failure is only a very ugly event. It can be a defining moment in the direction of your life, but it should not be the definition of you as a person.

I learned that they can take away your "stuff," (unless it was paid for, it really wasn't yours anyway) but there are also things that cannot be taken from you…things that only you can give away. These are life values like integrity. I believe that integrity can be likened to the purity of the soul. It's the one pure thing in each of us, the very fiber of our goodness. No one can take away your ethics, honesty, or integrity. But if you make the choice to give them away, chances are they're not coming back. In business, as well as in life, what defines us is not if we fail, but rather how we handle failure and its effects on us and those around us.

Here are some other things that I learned on my journey through failure:

- As Mom told me, "Sometimes life is too serious to take seriously." Try to keep your sense of humor in tough times; it may be your only link to sanity.

- The best of times bring nothing but joy. The worst of times bring out the best in good people and the worst in bad people, identifying each for who they really are.

- Family is the most important thing in our lives. The laughing, the loving, the caring and sharing of a family is the greatest success a person can attain. It's the real stuff. Talk to those you love, share your gains and your pains.

- Work hard to build your successful business, but get your priorities straight. No one ever said on their death bed, "Gee, I wish I had spent more time at the office."

- Call your mom and tell her you love her, then call her back and tell her again.

- Life has ups and downs. Always be nice to people on the way up, because you may be seeing them on the way down.

- Get Over Yourself. As bad as things are, there are others who have it worse.

- Don't take failure personally. I did and it nearly killed me. I kept my pain inside for ten years before I could speak of it. I was wrong. Is it tough? No, it's total Hell, but you can go on. Learn from me and get on with your life, now.

- So you won and the lost? Keep going for it. It's better to be a "Has Been" than a "Never Was."

And finally, I learned that we all fail and will continue to fail. It is part of the game of life.

Thomas Edison was ridiculed as he failed a remarkable ten thousand times before perfecting the incandescent light bulb.

Bath Ruth also held the major league record for strikeouts.

I think author Tom Hopkins said it best, *"I am not judged by the number of times that I fail, but by the number of times that I succeed. And the number of times that I succeed is in direct proportion to the number of times that I fail and keep trying."*

I'm not a professional writer, I'm just a businessman with a story to tell. *PUSHING WATER UPHILL With A Rake* is my story of chasing the American Dream. If, in reading my story, an attitude is changed, or a dialogue is opened between two people that are experiencing failure and a relationship is saved, then I have achieved success and in that I will take great pride.

I wish you all success.

Contact Steve Baker to speak to
your company, organization, or school.

How To Be
A Successful Failure

Steve shares the fun and excitement of
creating an extremely successful business and
the shock pain and despair as he watched it
all explode. It's about winning, losing, and
succeeding in business and in life.

Triangle Leadership™

From his forthcoming book, Steve shows
how you can become the most effective leader
possible, and how to create the future leaders
in your company. Steve's proven technique will
also help your family grow in a positive path.

*"Steve Baker has spoken to many of our
Kiwanis Clubs and he is dynamic! He kept our
audiences mesmerized as he combined wit and
wisdom to share his story along with his
philosophy on business, and the business of life.
He made us laugh and think.*
*Our clubs thoroughly enjoyed Steve and can't
wait to have him back."*

*- Mary Villalba, Governor,
Rocky Mountain District Kiwanis*

**Email Steve Baker at
PushingWaterUphill@earthlink.net**